Z.

DIGGIN' IN & PIGGIN' OUT

DIGGIN' IN AND PIGGIN' OUT

THE TRUTH ABOUT FOOD AND MEN

ROGER
WELSCH

HarperCollins*Publishers*

HarperCollins books may be purchased for educational, business, or sales promotional use. For information please write: Special Markets Department, HarperCollins Publishers, Inc., 10 East 53rd Street, New York, NY 10022.

FIRST EDITION

Designed by Joseph Rutt

Library of Congress Cataloging-in-Publication Data

Welsch, Roger L.
    Diggin' in and piggin' out : the truth about food and men /
Roger Welsch. — 1st ed.
        p.   cm.
    ISBN 0-06-018717-4
    1. Cookery. 2. Cookery—Humor. 3. Men—Humor.   I. Title.
TX652.W398   1997
641'.0207—dc20   96-44627

---

97 98 99 00 01 ❖/RRD 10 9 8 7 6 5 4 3 2 1

Dedicated to my mother, who I sincerely hope will read no further

"It's not so much that we are what we eat
as that we eat what we are."

—GEORGE SCHWELLE, *Visions*

UNPUBLISHED MANUSCRIPT, 1995

CONTENTS

FOREWORD

HIGH ON THE HOG

Roger Welsch does not keep himself at a contemporary distance from the sources of his food. I'm sure he's held a weanling pig on his lap for a chat, helped pull a calf during a difficult birth, and chased a rooster out of a flower bed. Part of a rooster's manhood is to do what you don't want him to do all the while pretending you are beneath his contempt. Roosters are the thugs of the barnyard, and there is a specific, literary strain in feeling endeared to them.

Following the lead of Umberto Eco, I have watched since my somewhat rural youth (my father was a country agricultural agent) as food has become an abstract imitation of what it once was. All blow and no show, as it were. The most recurrent phrase in both current food magazines and newspaper sections is "skinless, boneless, chicken breast." Many politically correct ninnies like to stay as far as possible from what we used to call the hind end of the bird. A skinless, boneless chicken breast carved from a hothouse factory chicken is the moral equivalent of Internet sex. But such is the nature of our prolonged urban drift that the majority of our population has never known an actual chicken, cow, or pig, or spent long summer afternoons hoeing a garden to grow vegetables that are still redolent of our mother, the earth.

In *Diggin' In and Piggin' Out*, Welsch, a renowned anthropologist and folklorist, explores the foibles of men at the table and stove. It is a highly amusing book and often a tad embarrassing for one who assumes he knows everything about the subject. I have often thought that anthropology should be taught rigorously in secondary school beginning as early as the seventh grade, so we can know what we actually are rather than live out so many banal assumptions. Welsch is humorously true to his discipline, grabbing us by our vain necks and showing us that some of our more pompous idiosyncrasies have a clearly discernible pattern.

This is a particularly male book, but it is well beyond any of the otiose dimensions of what is now called sexism. Women will like it, filling up, as it does, their ammunition canisters, giving them a rather lucid view of the decidedly primate habits of their partners. Men, particularly in locales well off the freeway, still tend to think that being a trencherman is something wonderful, on the order of, say, being a sports hero. Welsch quotes a comment by Jack Nicholson, who, after I had cooked a merry spread of fifty pounds of prime beef ribs at his house, said to me, "Only in the Midwest is overeating still considered an act of heroism." Once in an interview in *Women's Wear Daily* (of all places) I admitted that a small group of us had destroyed the evidence of an illegal deer by eating the entire creature in one day. We were pleased, as the game warden was unlikely to test stool samples. This would not be considered odd behavior in northern Michigan or in Nebraska, though it was received as such in Gotham. It might also have a causal relationship to my gout, come to think of it. The fact that this was possibly stupid behavior has not been lost on me. Welsch would regard the foolishness nonjudgmentally, in the manner of an educated dog.

Nebraska is a puzzle to nearly all but its inhabitants, and probably to most of those. Despite a dozen trips—some prolonged—to do research, I am scarcely an authority on the area, which is really two states: Lincoln and Omaha, and then all of the rest; in addition, under another schemata, one half of the state is specifically western, and the other half owns the peculiarities of the Midwest. Of course, the entire heartland is what film executives refer to as flyover country. I am a novelist and see and write what I wish to see and write, and have been relentlessly told about the "real" Nebraska, the "real" Montana, not to speak of the "real" France. I like to reply with Eric Erickson's prescient contention that reality is mankind's greatest illusion. The times have never been more contentious, and it behooves us not to put up with anyone's xenophobia. I've traveled by car through every state in the Union and have run through several dozen places that are earnestly, albeit weakly, described by their citizens as "God's country."

Welsch's farm sits by a muddy creek outside a small community named Dannebrog, the area straddling an imaginary lateral line between the Midwest and the West. East of here the folks are fatter, and if you go farther west into the Sandhills the people appear to be leaner and taller. Welsch himself is quite tall but decidedly not lean. (Like many real big folks, if he loses a few pounds he tends to think of himself as sprightly.) If you read all the wonderful recipes in this book, you'll see that they provide a nutritionist's nightmare, as they should: many of their origins were intended to feed people who were physically active in their jobs. You see a lot of grainbelt monsters in Eric's Tavern in Dannebrog that could squeeze Mike Tyson lifeless in a trice. They do not shrink from the table like California whippets, and all of this is to say that Welsch has not minced on the periphery of his subject. There is a reason he wears bib overalls daily. He has shown me the large closet containing forty-eight neatly stacked, well-worn pairs, each holding a particular subtle personality—or so he says. The man is a crank, and one can almost imagine him out in his barbecue shack roasting an entire Holstein udder, but then my research tells me this organ is eaten very rarely except by, you guessed it, the French, though American udders doubtless find their way into hot dogs.

The Nebraskan idea of food fiber tends to be Jell-O (or so one would think from their salad bars with their sparkling sneeze shields). Luckily for the traveler, this multicolored mud bath can be followed by the finest beef in God's creation. I can think of a number of places in the state where the beef is the equal of the fine steakhouses of Chicago and New York at about one-third of the price, so you can easily afford to eat more than one. One of the food curiosities one finds is the fabled *runza*, a simple, portable hamburger, cabbage, and potato pie. At a Lincoln *runza* bistro I had one served to me by a gorgeous cheerleader on roller skates, a sight to knock the James Joyce out of me. Just down the street from the fifth floor of the federal building an archaeologist I know mentioned the frequency of big Nebraskans who eat while they walk. Also, they tend to attack only one item at once, traveling clockwise around their plates as if settling the fate of nations.

There is a problem here, at which Welsch mildly hints and which can be thought as the "deer-crossing-the-highway syndrome." In a hundred years of the auto, deer and many other critters have lacked the evolutionary biology sufficient to avoid getting smacked by cars. In agrarian areas, such as Nebraska, many folks eat as if they had spent the day at the end of a hoe or shovel, or were still ploughing with horses. Welsch's book is full of what Julia Child meant when she referred to cassoulet as linebacker food. It is the kind of food I am genetically predisposed to eating daily even though I fear blowing up like a human version of the *Hindenburg*.

In other words, we are frequently the kind of deer that has not figured out cars. This notion wears an additional tail called Christian Fat, wherein reasonably devout men eat a lot and get big and fat in order to become unattractive, thus avoiding adultery; but then we'll leave that one to the cultural anthropologists.

The subtitle of *Diggin' In and Piggin' Out* is "The Truth About Food and Men." Pleasantly enough, and in the manner of Mark Twain, Welsch wins his points with a great deal of humor. Anthropologists and folklorists manage to conceal an enormous amount of valuable information by burying it deep in bad writing. For instance, one can slug one's way through the great Clifford Geertz because he writes well, while dozens of his colleagues in the profession should be send back to ninth-grade composition. Welsch writes very well indeed, so that the information is doubtless more digestible than the copious sidebar recipes.

Perhaps our appetites are a great deal more fated than we might wish, thus the nearly 100 percent rate of recidivism in diets that aren't accompanied by (and continued until death) exercise. Beneath the skin of many gourmets I know lurks a gourmand, or glutton, myself included. After several days of *haute cuisine* in Paris I like to sneak off to the Lipp for herring, roast chicken, and pommes frites, or to Thoumieux for *tête de veau* (made out of the head of a calf), or a simple stew of coxcombs and kidneys, with a salad of sliced chicken gizzards, lettuce, and chestnuts. Nebraska is the only other place I know where you can get excellent gizzards with a side of young bull nuts. What more could you possibly want, other than some Rolaids? Roger Welsch, in vulgar parlance, can not only talk the talk, he can walk the walk. The only part of Christmas I look forward to, with my big brown face pressed to the window, is the FedEx arrival of the ham from Welsch's backyard smokehouse. It is the food of my ever more distant youth.

Jim Harrison
Lake Leelanau, Michigan

INTRODUCTION

God sends meat, and the devil sends cooks.
—JOHN TAYLOR, 1630

'Tis an ill cook that cannot lick his own fingers.
—SHAKESPEARE,
Romeo and Juliet, 1594

A substantial proportion of the world's great cooks are men, and there's a reason for that. Men are *meant* to cook. Food and men go hand in hand, which can be messy in the case of dishes like chili, but . . . The secret is, however they may feel about *cooking*, men like to eat.

So, why are men no longer at home in the kitchens of their own homes? Why do so many men these days shrug their shoulders when it comes to mealtime and mutter something about not knowing how to boil water? I'll tell you why: it's a matter of a great and unnecessary disjuncture between man and his inner chef. Mister, you have it in you to cook, and this slim volume will get you back on track if anything can.

So, if I'm such a great cook, why haven't you heard of me before? Because I'm not such a great cook. Besides, who said anything about being a *great* cook? I'm talking about plain old *adequacy* here.

In fact, I'm not even talking about cooking; I'm talking about eating. And all you have to do is take one look at me to tell I know what I'm talking about when it comes to eating. In fact, some people say I'm a walking, talking advertisement for American agriculture, maybe world agriculture. As far as I can recall, I've eaten kangaroo, rattlesnake, turtle, shark, bear, dog, swordfish, ants, mescal worms (au jus), eel, beaver, muskrat, squirrel, horse, jackrabbit, goat, cottontail, blind robins, turtle eggs, ostrich, buffalo, deer, antelope, eland, clams, oysters, anemone, squid, octopus, shrimp, crab, lobster, seal, abalone, mussels, sea urchins, snails, God only knows what kinds of fish, including whale (yeah, smarty, I know whales are mammals)—and those are only the entrées.

There's 125-year-old wine and moonshine, still warm, dripping from the copper tube at the bottom of the still. Raw sugarcane at bullfights, juice from grapevines, sap from maple trees. Ants, minnows, grunion, armadillo, peccary, on and on and on.

I was once considered an expert in the area of edible wild plants, so I've done away with bushels of poke salad, dandelions, Jerusalem artichokes, groundnuts, puffballs, shelf fungi, smut, milkweed, nettles, sumac, sour dock, smart weed, daylilies, cattails, arrowhead, hackberries, gayfeather (watch your language, buddy!), sedge, ground cherries, sand cherries, chokecherries. . . . Never mind all the stuff on menus; I've gorged myself on mountain oysters (testicles), turkey fries (more testicles), sweetbreads (thymus glands), blood soup, bone marrow butter, tripe, buffalo gut, fried brains, head cheese, pig's feet, kidneys, liver, heart, tongue, oxtail, and ox neck, to tie ends together.

Get this: I've even eaten Twinkies, Slim Jims, and tapioca pudding. I consider myself om-damn-niver-ous.

I've been married, and I've been single; I've been young, and I've been old; I've cooked in the sunshine and in the rain, in an open canoe and in a tent, in the snow and in a windstorm, inside and outside, over a house fire, and over a candle. I've eaten Indian food, Tibetan food, Eskimo food, cowboy food, Lapp food, Egyptian food, Nigerian food, Pilgrim food, army food, *real* Mexican food, *Mayan* food.

Yes, I've cooked some pretty bad food, but I've paid some pretty good money for bad food, too. In fact, I'd guess that some of the worst meals I've had in my life were also some of the most expensive. Some of the best food I've ever eaten, on the other hand, has been some of the cheapest— and the simplest. In fact, some of the best meals I've ever enjoyed were put together out of some of the worst food I've ever eaten.

So, how does that make any sense at all? Let me give you two frinstances.

CASE STUDY IN BAD FOOD/GOOD MEAL SYNDROME #1

I was floating down the Platte River with a good buddy, who has since passed away. (He's alive; it's just that he's passed away.) It was not an altogether idyllic voyage. The first day had gone well, and that, as it turned out, is where everything went wrong. It was a sunny, warm day with little wind and a perfect temperature for late April. We were looking for morel mushrooms and wild asparagus and having some modest success finding both.

As we rounded a bend of a sandy island, we spotted two huge snapping turtles sitting right at the water's edge, an unusual adventure for snappers. As we slipped by the sandbar, the turtles, remarkably, didn't dive into the water. Insanely, my buddy reached out with lightning speed (a snapper can take off a finger easily and will inflict crippling wounds, given a chance), grabbed a tail, and flipped one of the turtles into the boat, where it proceeded to demolish coolers, sleeping bags, clothing, and other equipment. Didn't matter. We had an entrée for a great camp supper.

We were about ready to consider settling in for the night. Although it was still fairly early in the evening, we were in no hurry and there was no reason to push. The stretch of Platte we were enjoying is clogged with thousands of islands, ranging in size from hundreds of acres to not much bigger than a living-room couch. We spotted a nice clearing on an island a couple acres large and pulled up to a nice landing spot, stepping from my old, aluminum, flat-bottom scow onto . . . a bed of morel mushrooms in prime shape. We had to be careful to pick the ground clean before we set up our camp. We wound up with maybe two bushels of the lovelies.

Except along the edges of the island, which were crowded with fresh, firm young asparagus spears instead of morel mushrooms. Again, far more than we could eat. I pulled some selected greens (mostly sour dock) for a salad and spotted near the edge of a nearby spring . . . my God, watercress! We were set for a salad fit for a king. My pal came from a short inland visit carrying some sprigs; "What's this?" he asked, and they were some of the prettiest peppermint plants I've ever seen. We were set for a remarkable evening, with an après-dinner tea, on top of everything else.

We had butter for our asparagus, although we gorged

ourselves on it raw, it was so succulent. Our salad was crispy and tart. We had clear water with bruised peppermint to cleanse our palates, and then a little Jack Daniel's to warm the chill of the evening. I sautéed bits of snapping turtle and morels in a frying pan with butter, all we could eat. The evening was so gorgeous; we couldn't remember another like it. Everything was perfect. We heard a loon . . . the only loon I've heard in my sixty years of life. Is this magic? It was from that friend I learned that anything worth doing is worth overdoing, and that night we followed his philosophy in spades. We ate too much, drank too much, laughed too much. We closed the night with hot peppermint tea. We crawled into our sleeping bags—the night was way too perfect for a tent—and we went to sleep utterly stuffed, utterly content.

The next morning we discovered anew the consequences of debauchery, just as humans have done, so far as I can tell, throughout all time, without permanent education. I was desperately ill from all that food and drink. My friend, fifteen years younger, was a lot better, except that he discovered as we broke camp that he had left the keys for the car we were floating toward at the end of our trip in the car we had left the day before at the beginning of our trip. In other words, we had no transportation at the end of our voyage. Ah well, that's another day, we decided, and besides, we're sick enough right now that maybe we should concentrate on just getting back onto the—choke, gag—water.

Actually, it wasn't all that bad. It got bad an hour later when it started to rain real good. And the wind picked up. And we got caught in a shallow channel and wound up dragging the damned boat and all our equipment for miles across moist sand. And finally, exhausted, we decided it was time to make camp again.

This time there were no morels, no asparagus, no snapping turtle stew, no mint tea. In fact, there was also no campfire. Our matches were soaked, but then so was any firewood we could find, and the place where we decided to collapse for the night wouldn't have allowed a campfire anyway. We stopped by another island, but this one was not so easy to get up onto. It had high banks, which we decided might be for the best if the water should start rising during the night. What turned out to be magic about this place, however, was that right at the edge of the island we found a gigantic old red cedar tree (actually a juniper, but in Nebraska we call them red cedars).

I won't go into the whole issue, but old trees (and therefore *big* trees) are something of a rarity in Nebraska. One of the principal factors that kept the Nebraska prairie the Nebraska prairie was fire. Grass fires annually swept across the Plains at lightning speed, sometimes the result of escaped campfires, from Indians long before settlers, earlier still from lightning, and later from trains. Trees were a rarity when the homesteaders came, and they still are. Old ones are very rare. Except, as I learned later, on some of the islands of the Platte, where fire (and another arboreal ravager, the bison) couldn't reach them. And this must have been one of the elders.

The tree was huge. (I wince as I write that in the past tense, because I hope with all my heart that that tree still prospers.) Under its lowest boughs was a large, clear, clean floor strewn with a soft, ancient bed of needles. (See? No fire.) The opening was almost large enough to stand in. The trunk was gigantic and gnarled, a wonderful backrest. By now it was raining and blowing ferociously, but in that tree's bosom it was quiet, dry, and warm. *This* was the magic. Not the fancy meal with all the good foods and the perfect night, but this, a miserable night at the heart of this old tree, drenched in its perfume and soul. We were hungover, dirty, tired, and hungry, but we ate what humble stuff we had—some sardines and white bread, crackers and Cheez Whiz, warm water.

As tired as we were, we didn't want to go to sleep because everything seemed so insanely comfortable under that tree. The rain poured off the tree's thatch but we were magically, mystically dry. Now, isn't that crazy? That was a great meal, not because of the food, but because of the company and the locale. That's how men eat. (Maybe women, too, but only women get to go to Woman School where they learn the things they know, so there's no way for me to know. They don't teach that stuff in Man School.)

CASE STUDY IN BAD FOOD/GOOD MEAL SYNDROME #2

I had recently met a young woman in one of my classes, younger than me but older than the conventional student. She was, in fact, a secretary in another of the school's departments, taking my courses on her way to a degree. On this occasion, she was taking a summer class of mine, a study of Plains literature and folklore, and she, maybe a dozen other eager students, and I were out in the middle of Nebraska, working like dogs, filling long days with study and discussion.

After several days together in our class, my attraction to the woman grew considerably stronger, even though by that time we hadn't even had much of a conversation outside classroom situations. In fact, every word we exchanged had come to seem a kind of coded romance. No doubt about it, this woman was not only gorgeous, but also intellectually fascinating, spiritually profound, personally warm, witty, bright, gentle—at this point, she had become all I could think of!

On the last day of the class we went to a small-town steak house for food and drink, a kind of graduation banquet. Well, as it wound up, I spent most of my time talking with some people I wasn't too eager to talk with, and I had to watch the woman I most wanted to talk with . . . if nothing else, just look into her sky-blue eyes . . . laughing with other students. God, while I was talking with some old folks who were telling me about how their children had gone off to become missionaries in Zimbabwe, I could hear her laughter, the most erotic thing about her, coming from the room with the music, dancing, and all those horny damned cowboys.

In this case the food was its usual okay, the beer was cold but not very interesting, the salad was soggy, nothing was right. Because the company and place were wrong. In fact, if I think about it real hard, I can recall that the meal was perfectly dreadful.

At that point.

In fact, I finally stomped out of the place, announcing that I was going and . . . uh . . . anyone who wanted a ride better come right now. And wham! That blue-eyed woman of my dreams was there as if I had rubbed a genie's lantern, leaving the cowboys in the back room wondering if they hadn't been dreaming. At some point everything tore loose with the subtlety of a tornado, and it became clear that I wasn't alone in my madness. We instantly became the only person in each other's lives, we got married and always will be. The woman was my Lovely Linda. And now that miserable damned meal is a legend to us, remembered and recounted again and again and again and again.

That's how men eat, and maybe women, too.

The bottom line is, this book isn't a cookbook, which I feel comfortable in telling you now that you've paid for it.

My original plan was to be *real* cute and have just one recipe in the whole thing, the one for Roger's Ribs, because I don't believe in recipes and nobody who loves food ever cooks from a cookbook. Okay, so there are quite a few recipes, as it turns out, in this book, but I have set them all off as sidebars, thus indicating in a literarily subtle way that they are peripheral to the main text, mostly a sop to the publisher.

Nor is this a gourmet guide to good eating. It's a book about men and food. I got a lot of flak about the title of a previous book, *Old Tractors and the Men Who Love Them* (Motorbooks International, Osceola, WI, 1995), because it appeared sexist. Thing is, I don't know how women love old tractors. I know there are women who do, but I don't know how their love feels, because I'm a man. Maybe I should have called this one *Foods and the Men Who Eat Them*. When the tractor book came out, I explained that it wasn't just for gearhead guys who work on rusty iron; I hoped that it would also help explain lugs like me to ladies like my Linda, and I have every indication that that's exactly what it did.

That's what I envision for this book too. Yeah, I know it looks and starts and maybe even ends like a book for males at their most basic, but I am only trying to explain how I feel about food, eating, and cooking. What I would really like to do is get a bunch of guys to read it and say, "Yeah, yeah, yeah, that's the way it is! Right, that's exactly how it goes. That's me. Uh-huh, that's my dad and me. Yep, yep, yep."

And then I'd like to get a bunch of women to read it and say, "Oh, is that how that big bozo feels? How sweet. Oh, the darling. Yes, that's exactly how that slob operates. God, what a jerk. But I do love him. Next time, maybe I'll let him marinade his damned ribs in the kitchen instead of out in the machine shed."

That's all I ask.

Well, almost all I ask. I also asked my mother not to read past the dedication page. There's a good reason for that. I asked her to read *Old Tractors and the Men Who Love Them,* because I wanted it to be readable, maybe even interesting to someone who's never so much as turned a screwdriver, and she hasn't. She told me later that she did truly enjoy the book . . . except . . . except . . . except, "I don't feel it is ever appropriate to use the 'f-word.'" I was stunned. I rarely use that word in speech and I certainly didn't mean to use it in the sacred text of my tractor book. I maintained my stunned silence as she went on, and as she did, I began to sort out the problem: she was talking about the passage in which I refer to myself as an "old fart." She was offended by my use of the word . . . *fart.*

Isn't that cute? That darling woman probably thinks that when they talk about the "f-word" on television or in print, that's what they have in mind—fart. Well, I use the word *fart* in this book, and probably a couple other words that might be offensive to her, and I adore her, so . . . Mom, if you've come *this* far, stop right now.

THE KITCHEN

One can become a cook, but one is born a roaster of meat.
—ANTHELME BRILLAT-SAVARIN,
Physiologie de goût, 1825

Kissing don't last; cookery do!
—GEORGE MEREDITH,
Ordeal of Richard Feverel, 1859

THE SHANGRI-LA RESTAURANT AND TOOL SHOP

My friend Jim Harrison is famous for his poetry and fiction, probably most of all for his novels that have been made into movies—*Wolf,* for example, or *Legends of the Fall.* I first saw his work in *Esquire* magazine, where he was foods columnist. The first time he came to visit our farm in the middle of Nowhere, Nebraska, Linda and I were both a little intimidated (although I don't intimidate easy). I mean, jeez, there are not a lot of gourmet spots around here, and Linda is one hell of a cook, but for the food columnist of *Esquire?!* Whew.

Well, as it turns out, Jim's taste is wide and eclectic. Maybe he's just kindhearted. Anyway, we didn't have any

1

problems, and we've learned to relax and let him eat what we eat. Which seems to be all he asks. But what I'm leading up to is that the first evening he spent with us, we were sitting around the fireplace, drinking some good single-malt Scotch, an Islay, as I recall. (I drink cheap beer, cheap wine, cheap vodka, cheap all sorts of things, and even prefer green label Jack Daniel's to the more expensive black label, but I *do* admire single-malt Scotch!) We talked about the region, my interest in good tools and antique tractors, that sort of thing. But eventually our conversation focused on food, probably at my instigation, because I was excited about talking food with this expert.

Finally, Jim spoke of his dream. A service station in town was for sale at the time, and Jim said he'd love to buy a place like that and turn it into the perfect dining spot. He said he would like to turn what was then the tire repair bay into a tool shop, where I could have the best available tools on display, maybe with an old tractor sitting there to test the tools on. Where cars were then being greased and tuned, Jim said he would develop his perfect eatery. There would be no menu. You would just come in and sit down, and a perfect meal for that week would be served—the best beef, the best fish, the best poultry, the best wine, the best beer, the best liquor, the best vegetables, the best bread, the best salads. All served by beautiful, completely naked young women. (He explained that he believes sanitation problems arise with foods where cloth, a notorious germ carrier, is involved.)

His eyes—or, at least, eye—rising to the ceiling, he said we could have a gorgeous plate of hors d'oeuvres, maybe some snails in garlic butter (*drawn* butter), with French bread, and then, excusing ourselves from the naked waitresses, adjourn briefly to the tool room to admire the latest edition of combination wrenches from Snap-on as compared with

Craftsman's professional series. Maybe we could sip an aperitif.

Then back to the table and the naked ladies for salad and soup, perhaps a sorbet to cleanse our palates, and a finger bowl to take care of the tractor grease we might have picked up in the tool room. And a light white wine for the salad course. A California selection would be fine.

Well, our conversation went pretty much along that line until Jim stopped, picked up his Scotch, looked at me seriously (with his *good* eye), and said, "Rog, sure as hell you put together a great place like that, you know they're going to make you open it to the public."

Jay Leno has said that he would like to open a "guy's restaurant," where you would eat straight out of the can, leaning over a sink. For most men, that would work just fine.

ON THE RUN, IN THE SUN

I used to drive a 1969 Chevy van, the one with all the body styling of a Nabisco Shredded Wheat box. The engine in this beast was in a big iron box right between the driver and the passenger seats, which offered a number of advantages. For example, when I had engine trouble, which was often, I could always work on it indoors.

Best of all, however, I cooked on it. I could just pop open the top of the engine compartment while buzzing down a highway at fifty-five miles an hour, and there was the engine, roaring away, all hot and toasty. Before setting off on my trip I would put some things like leftover pizza or hamburgers in aluminum foil packets, which I then plunked down, right on top of the engine—the stuff that needed the hottest temperatures up against the manifold, that which needed less heat back on the block. An hour later I would open the engine box again, and there were my sandwiches or pizza, nicely warmed. That's all a man needs by way of a kitchen.

This is a book about men and food, so I don't want to drag women into this operation, except where absolutely necessary and then only for purposes of comparison, but it's definitely my impression that women are a little more, uh, particular when it comes to kitchens. For example, when my wife and I first moved into our house, we were still working out the basic ground rules for life in it. I came home one day with some catfish I had caught in the river and cleaned them in what seemed to me the most logical possible place, the kitchen sink. And I cleaned up the mess afterward, knowing Linda would want her new kitchen to be the way she left it, which is to say, immaculate. Unfortunately, she spotted an insignificant pool of fish blood under the toaster and, casting her eyes heavenward in despair, spotted a few minor spots of fish guts on the ceiling.

As if they were that obvious or anything. And it's not as if I put them there on purpose. Despite my rational explanations and fervent pleas, I was officially and immediately banned from the kitchen for fish-cleaning purposes. She let me continue to cook my ribs and secret sauce in her kitchen until she found some of that secret sauce dripping off the counter into the silverware drawer, which was open ever so slightly, where it was dissolving some of our stainless-steel flatware. And she began telling friends, neighbors, and folks she ran into at the Kmart that every time I cooked ribs, she had to repaint the kitchen.

Did I sulk? Did I pout? Did I complain? No, I did not. *I built myself a summer kitchen in the backyard.*

My summer kitchen is only ten by twelve feet, but it is mine, and the sign on the door says NO GURLS. The floor is linoleum so I can hose it off after a particularly vigorous cooking session. The stove is an old wood-burning laundry stove. (Men cook best over fire, I find.) I have an old enameled tin table and a wall cupboard where I keep utensils—well, okay, a big fork, a big spoon, and a big knife—and other kitchen necessaries: *Penthouse* magazines, a bottle of Jack Daniel's green label, bandages, and burn ointment. There are metal buckets for beer cans and soaking woods I use in smoking meats, racks of apple, mesquite, and hickory wood for smoking, big old iron pots and Dutch ovens, and a chair, so I can sit down whilst stirring the soup and petting my black Labs when they come visiting. I spend long hours in my summer kitchen, nursing along a mess of ribs, thumbing through a, uh, literary magazine, sucking at a gin and tonic, looking out the open door, watching the clouds in the sky ("If you look through one eye and squint a little with the other, doesn't that cloud over there look just like Claudia Schiffer?"). Now, that, I submit, is a kitchen.

Recipe for the Best Ribs in the World, or at Least in Dannebrog, Nebraska

ROGER'S GIN AND TONIC RIBS

Select meaty ribs—spare, country-style, beef, pork, or possum, doesn't matter. Several days in advance of cooking, put quart of good gin (this is not the time to be cheap; save the cheap gin for in-laws) in the freezer and several bottles of Schweppe's tonic water in the refrigerator. Obtain several fresh limes.

The day before cooking the ribs, prepare a marinade of a quart or two of wine vinegar (I have used fresh beer or wine—I like red—but I really do prefer the taste of vinegar), a couple bottles of ranch-style salad dressing (no kidding), and Tabasco sauce, season salt, and garlic to taste. Put aside to "mingle" for a day. If the ribs are frozen, remove them from the freezer so they are thoroughly thawed before your cooking day begins.

The next day, put aside plenty of time for cooking the ribs. This is not a task frivolously dismissed. Rib days for me start shortly after noon. Soak a couple handfuls of good smoking wood (I like mesquite, apple, mulberry, or cobs—or, if you can get it, hunks of such woods just small enough to fit into your smoker) in a can or bucket of water. If you are using larger hunks of wood, start soaking them the day before, right after preparing the marinade. Slice two limes into quarter sections.

Take a very large container, along the line of one of those big, insulated covered coffee mugs you pick up at a quick-stop gas-and-food joint, and fill it with ice cubes. (If you really want to be smart, take a couple empty frozen orange juice containers—those paper "cans" about the size of a breakfast juice glass, fill them with water several days before you start cooking the ribs, and put them in the freezer with the gin; that will give you *big* cubes that outlast little ones ten to one. You just peel the paper "can" away from the big cube.)

Bring a large pot of water to a boil and drop the ribs into it. Boil the ribs only ten minutes or so (depending on size; some country-style ribs take fifteen minutes)—not long enough that the meat becomes loose from the bone but long enough that the meat is hot throughout. The liqueur you take from the ribs makes superb soup when bits of pork or ham, small pasta or rice, and seasoning are added.

Place hot ribs in deep container of marinade so they are completely covered. Now pour several ounces of frozen gin over the cup of ice. Bruise two lime slices and add to gin and ice. Pour enough tonic water over mixture to bring to top of cup. Put cover carefully on cup, taking care not to spill.

Take this mixture to site of cooking. Start coals in smoker or backyard grill a good half hour before you plan to begin barbecuing the ribs. When the coals of your fire are thoroughly aglow, drain the ribs of excess barbecue sauce, sprinkle soaked wood chips on coals, and put ribs on grill well above the coals—as high as your grill or smoker allows. (You've pretty much cooked the ribs in the boiling water; now you're just finishing the job, letting fats cook off, and adding a wonderful smoke flavor, so there's no need to hurry at this point, and, as you will see, considerable reason for a measured pace.)

Stretch a hammock between two appropriately spaced trees *upwind* from the grill, if you have not already had the foresight to do so. Sip at your frozen gin and tonic throughout the process. Watch smoke curl into the sky from your grill, preferably in the company of a good, big black dog. Throw a Frisbee for the dog. Sip your gin and tonic. Think about people who live in Los Angeles and New York. Try to find clouds that look like Cindy Crawford or any of her various parts. Sip gin and tonic. Keep busy. Well, more precisely, keep busy looking like you're busy.

Important:

Open cooker and check the ribs occasionally so no one in the house thinks you're just loafing. Make noises by clattering barbecue tools and cooker. Intently examine a sample rib now and then. At all times, continue to insist you are cooking and cannot afford to lose your focus by pruning bushes or mowing the lawn or baby-sitting a child. Fuss with fire, add chips, doctor gin and tonic.

Turn ribs occasionally; sprinkle more wet wood chips on fire. Be sure gin and tonic level does not drop below half full or a loss of the efficiency of the balance of ice, tonic, gin, and lime may result. Add ice cubes and lime slices when necessary. When properly timed, this process can pretty much eat up an afternoon. The wood-chip smoke not only flavors the meat but keeps flies, children, and wives away from the hammock when properly placed.

Sample ribs frequently, clearing palate with gin and tonic. When the meat is thoroughly cooked and has a nice crispy finish, refresh gin and tonic and baste the tops of the ribs with your favorite barbecue sauce. Frankly, it doesn't matter which. A good gin and Schweppe's tonic water is a lot more important than the kind of barbecue sauce you use, believe me. If you do this right, you could use catsup and nobody would notice.

Let the ribs cook on the grill another ten minutes or so. Don't hesitate to add more wood chips to the fire or gin and tonic to the ice cup. Turn ribs and baste once more. Time the last basting and turning of the ribs so that your gin and tonic runs out just as you lift the ribs off the grill. This saves a trip into the house.

Call wife and kids to table. Serve ribs. Accept praise modestly. Let someone else do the dishes. Retreat in exhaustion to the couch. Have someone rub your shoulders.

Have another gin and tonic. You've earned it.

Most of my indoor cooking is restricted to our fireplace. I have done some stews in Dutch ovens in the coals of our hearth, but best of all, I like to grill steaks and wienies over the fire in the winter. They taste better, and it's more fun.

And men are supposed to cook over open fire. Who cooks over the barbecue grill? Men, that's who. Because it's fundamental, that's why. Steaks cooked any other way than on the grill over real charcoal constitutes gastronomic abuse, in my opinion. In our backyard, in front of the summer kitchen (where I also keep all my barbecue grill equipment, supplies, and a small smoker), are our grill, an old metal table, and my hammock, right under a nice cottonwood tree. Now, that's a man's kitchen.

Steak

What's to know, right? You take the meat, throw it over a charcoal fire, take it off, and eat it! Nah, there's a little more to it than that. First of all, the best steaks for barbecuing are thick steaks. Barbecuing dries meat, so thick slabs allow for a crispy, dry outside but a juicy inside. Sometimes, when I don't have a lot of time, however, I grab a thinnish steak because it will cook in a matter of moments over a hot fire. If you are starting with frozen meat, be darned sure it is thoroughly thawed before you toss it on the grill. And your coals should be at their hottest when you throw on the steaks, not just starting to burn.

By the way, I like to start my cooking fires with an electric coal starter (I found mine at Sears) rather than liquid starter and matches. I can't help but think that kerosene stuff lends an off flavor to food. I like the square, flattish grills you can close down tight and which have variable height settings for the grill itself. I am not at all fond of the ball-shaped ones where your meat is a long ways from the heat. I can't imagine cooking over a *gas* fire outdoors any more than I would boil a filet, but some people I respect do exactly that, and I have always argued that what men do in the privacy of their patio is their own business, so. . . .

I put my steaks over the fire with the grill at its lowest setting, the meat close to the heat. I leave it there only a minute or so to sear the meat and seal in the juices. Then I raise the grill about midway above the coals. *The real secret to cooking steak or burgers on the grill is to turn the meat only once.* It breaks my heart to see someone flipping, flipping, flipping that meat, losing precious juices—and flavor—with every flip. Leave the meat over the heat until juices just begin to come through the top; at this point your meat is rare. When it is coming through generously and pooling, the meat is medium. Don't ask me for advice if you are cooking good meat to the point of being well done; that should be a crime punishable by vegetarianism. Jeez, well done!

Now, turn the meat, set the grill low for just a quarter to a half minute, raise the grill, and let her cook until juice begins to come through again, which won't be as long this time.

SMOKIN'

My other cooking sites are a smokehouse, an old refrigerator converted to a large smoker, and an open fire pit, a ways away from the house, in front of a cabin I have down by the river. The smokehouse was originally built a full century ago, and I moved it here twenty years ago when I first bought the farm. It is eight by ten feet and is a typical farm smokehouse. It has a door but no windows or other openings. Across the tops of the walls are six heavy poles with wire hooks, from which I hang hams and bacon when I do my annual smoke, sometime around mid-December. On the sand floor, directly in the middle of the building, there is a firebox from an old woodstove. And that's all there is to it.

Hams

I got started doing my own hams when I was still doing my own butchering, which I got into when I found my city-born and -bred children didn't know where their food was coming from. I think we were having pork chops one evening when one of them asked me what "chops" are and what's a "pork"? Good question. You know, a half-dozen centuries ago the rich nobles of England were Normans, and they spoke French. The poor slobs out on the farms were Anglo-Saxons and they spoke a Germanic language. English is now a combination of both those languages and a few others.

Anyway, the Germanic farmers raised the animals and they called them by good ol' Anglo-Saxon words—*swine, cows, sheep, calves.* The rich Normans who ate the meat called it by the French words for those animals—*porq, boeuf, mutton, veal*. Add fancy supermarket packaging to that, and it's not easy for people to know what it is they're eating today. So, I explained, "Well, chops are like T-bone steaks, except they're from a pig."

Well, that caused something of a sensation at our supper table, what with the kids making hacking and gagging sounds and me snarling that the least we can do is be grateful to the animals that give their lives so we can eat. Time for education, I thought, and a couple weekends later, I took the kids out to a farm to help me butcher a hog (and I wonder why my youngest daughter of that family is a vegetarian?). I cut the hog up for the freezer and cured and eventually smoked the two front shoulder hams, the two large rear hams, and the bacon.

Now it was time for me to be surprised. I had been eating waterlogged commercial hams so long, I had forgotten how wonderful *real* ham could be. These days I no longer do my own butchering, but I do smoke a mess of hams every Christmas for gifts and for our own freezer. I just go to our local grocer and have him order me thirty or forty shoulder hams and a half-dozen larger rear hams, and maybe a bacon slab or two—uncured, unsmoked. If you try this, you may be surprised to find that you'll pay pretty much the same for uncured, unsmoked meat as you do for finished hams and bacon. The difference is that the finished hams are heavily injected with water and you're paying for a pound or two of water with every commercial ham.

I use a commercial cure (Morton's Tender Quick curing compound), which is nothing more than salt, saltpeter (no, it won't, no matter what they told you in the army), and maybe a little sugar. I mix the commercial cure with a few pounds of brown sugar, maybe a little molasses to help it stick, and a couple bottles of Tabasco hot sauce. On a cool-to-cold day, I haul everything out to my shop and start the process. I poke a hole through the shank of each ham and pass a wire or cord through so I can hang the ham later in the smokehouse. Then I rub each ham thoroughly with cure and put it into a clean plastic garbage can. I use gigantic cans because I do a mess of meat at a time. I pierce, rub, and pack hams pretty much all day like this, and when I'm done, I have three big barrels full of hams. I add just enough water to raise the liquid level to the top of the barrel. It doesn't take much.

I keep the shop at about 35°–40°, and every couple days I pull each ham out of the brine, rub it again, and put it back in the barrel. I've never figured out exactly how long to do this. Back in the old days they just salted the living bejesus out of hams. They didn't have freezers, so they planned on hanging those hams in the barn or tossing them into the oats bin for a year or so, and it took a lot of salt to keep them from going bad or drawing bugs. Then they had to boil the hams for days to get enough salt out to make them edible again.

I don't have to do that. All I want to do is have the cure penetrate through the meat, right to the bone. The cure is what turns a pork butt into a ham. It gives the meat that reddish color and lends flavor. too. (You can do the same thing with turkeys!) Some people use a large syringe to inject cure into the meat, but I've never been very successful at that. So I just soak. And I guess at how I'm doing. Last year the weather was too warm to fire up the smokehouse, so I kept the hams in the cure solution almost two weeks. It was too long. The hams were a little too salty and therefore required a little extra boiling time. Once I had only five or six days; that wasn't long enough, which means that deep in the ham, near the bone, the meat cooked brown instead of red and tasted like roast pork rather than ham. No big deal, but still . . .

On a cold day, I haul the hams down to the smokehouse, usually with a tractor if there's snow. This is the fun part. There's nothing prettier than a smokehouse full of hams. Thing is, you're not cooking the hams at this point. In fact, you want them to stay nice and cold so they don't get rancid or spoil. All you're doing is adding a little bit of a new flavor— smoke. I hang the hams from the poles in the smokehouse and light my smudge.

I like apple wood and cobs. Cobs make a delicious, sweet smoke. I take big hunks of apple wood— sometimes I wet them a little so they'll burn more slowly and smoke more—and pack them into the iron tub of the stove in the middle of the smokehouse. I start the fire with some finely split apple wood. I close the tub so it gets as little air as possible, and I close the door to the smokehouse. That's it. Four or five hours later I come back, restoke the smudge, and check to make sure everything's okay. Just before I go to bed, I build the smudge again, and as soon as I get up the next morning, I start the process again. I do this for four or five days. Yes, it gets to be a bit of a chore, but it's such a pretty thing to do, and it happens only once a year. I visit the smokehouse a minimum of three times a day— better yet, five or six.

I have also used cherry and pear wood and they

seem to be fine. A friend who doesn't have access to good fruitwood has used mulberry, which is abundant on the Plains, and he very much likes its flavor. This year I got some apricot wood, so I'm giving it a try.

On the last day, I take my garbage cans with me in the pickup truck or tractor and empty the poles in the smokehouse . . . and close it down for another year. It's a bit of a sad moment, actually. Each and every year I promise myself at this moment that when the weather is good next spring, I'll fix the hinges on the door, clean up the messy floor, close up some of the gaps between the walls and the stones they sit on, knock down some of the cobwebs . . . but I never do.

Now, here's more fun: We don't have room in our freezer to store all those hams until Christmas. So I take twenty or so of them in the back of my old blue Ford pickup truck and start making the rounds of all our friends, giving them a Christmas present a little early. All day long I visit friends and give them the products of the last week's work. Doesn't that sound like fun? It is. And that night, back at the house, we have ham for supper, just like Martha Stewart would.

And here's how Linda cooks it:

Scrub ham well. Place in a kettle of simmering water, cider, beer, or ginger ale. Simmer 20–30 minutes *per pound*. The thermometer will register 165° when the meat is done. This takes care of the actual cooking, but to make the ham look good at the table, let it partially cool in the liquid in which it was cooked. Drain. (The water from boiling the ham makes a terrific base for bean soup; just add beans and onions.) Strip off skin. Preheat oven to 425°.

Cover top of ham with brown sugar and a little dry mustard. Stud with whole cloves, if desired. Lower oven temperature to 325° and bake for about 20 minutes more. Baste with pineapple juice. Place pineapple slices on top and cook 30 minutes more. I like my ham with mustard . . . hot Coleman's mustard.

About midway between our house and the smokehouse, maybe a hundred yards from where I'm sitting as I write this, there is an old metal refrigerator with some bricks and an ancient, rusty iron frying pan in the bottom. I chopped a small hole in the back and secured a sheet metal flap over it with a small bolt so I can open and close it as a draft. This fridge smoker (don't try this with a plastic refrigerator!) is for hot smoking—mostly fish and poultry. (Hot smoking cooks food while it is flavored with smoke; hams and bacon, on the other hand, should stay cold while they bask in the rich smokes rising from the floor of the smokehouse.)

Turkey

When I smoke turkey in my refrigerator-transformed-into-a-smoker, the process is substantially different from how the smokehouse works because in the fridge, I am actually *cooking* the meat as it smokes. I poked some holes through the refrigerator box, near the top of the box, and ran some steel rebar through it. I take a fresh turkey and put it in an onion sack—you know, the loosely woven bags you buy twenty or so pounds of onions in. I got some of these from an onion factory not far from here. I wire the top of the bag together and use the wire to hang the bird from one of the lengths of rebar. (You can use this same process with chicken, fish, and probably just about any kind of meat.)

On the floor of the refrigerator box, I have a metal pan in which I place some barbecue charcoal, and I light it. Then I pack hunks of moist fruitwood around the coals—again, I like apple wood, but I have used pear, too. Four bricks sit on end in the corners of the refrigerator box and on top of them sits one of the old shelf racks from the fridge. On it, immediately above the fire pan, I place a light aluminum roasting pan full of water. Essentially, you are not so much baking the bird as you are *steaming* it. And that steam really carries the heat and flavor of the wood smudge to the meat. Moreover, the pan catches the dripping fat and juices from the bird, preventing flare fires or an extinguished smudge. This is not a real hot fire, so it takes pretty much most of a day for the bird to cook, but man, is it good!

(Two women in my life read this manuscript for me. Both insisted that I make a big fuss about making sure pork is thoroughly cooked, that there are such things as meat thermometers, that you can get worms, on and on and on. The fact of the matter is, if the brine and cure doesn't kill any ugly-buglies in the meat, and the smoking doesn't bother them, and the freezing doesn't blitz 'em but good, then the cooking will, and you don't have to boil the living bejesus out of it to make it safe. But here's my man-to-man advice: if you're going to have a woman around when you eat this stuff, tell her you cooked it for thirty hours at 560°.)

I realize there are certain problems—like fussy neighbors—with the notion of putting a nice old smokehouse or battered and smoky refrigerator in a suburban backyard. That's why I live on a farm. If you don't have neighbors, or, alternately, have neighbors you would really like to piss off, an old outhouse makes a dandy small smokehouse, with just enough room to hang four to eight hams. If you use a small structure like an outhouse, you may not want to build your smoke fire inside it—not so much because of fire danger as the necessity of keeping your hams cool as they smoke. (Warm pork is not a great thing for human beings, but I hear bacteria find it a lovely home.) In that case, what you want to do is get a small firebox of some kind—a barrel with a chimney will do, or even a fire pit with a few lengths of stove pipe leading to the smokehouse—and conduct cool smoke into the smokehouse in that manner.

Frankly, I can't imagine a real man without a still functioning outhouse, anyway. What do you do if you don't have an outhouse, for example, and it's a warm spring day, and you've been eating pickled boiled eggs and drinking beer, and the notion comes over you, if you catch my drift? I so enjoy my outhouse, I put a window in the west side so I can sit there and not only look out the door over the river bottoms but look to the west toward the setting sun or the migrating deer or the approaching tornadoes, depending on the season.

The best smokehouse I've ever seen is Lyle Fries's. He had it built special. It's brick and round. Inside, he had an old wagon axle set in the floor, with a steel wheel left on it. This way, he can open the door and hang hams on the lazy Susan inside, turning it as he adds hams. He has iron draft doors and a metal firebox as well as an outdoor firebox with plenty of stovepipe to let the smoke cool. It's beautiful. Maybe your neighbors wouldn't mind that. Tell 'em it's a chapel.

No, that's wrong. Lyle Fries's brick smokehouse is not the best smokehouse I've ever seen. The best smokehouse I've ever seen was in northern Germany, near the city of Kiel. I was staying with an anthropologist friend of mine on his farm. He was the kind of host everyone should have when visiting a foreign country. He knew that I would want to see what's typical of the area, so he made sure I visited a family for a typical rural German Christmas dinner— of carp, one of the lowliest fish in my home area of the Americas' Plains. (It was delicious: the farmer explained that when he fed his horses and cows and chickens every evening, he also tossed a bucket of corn into the pond where he kept his fish, thus "finishing" the fish just as a livestock grower here finishes beef by feeding cows corn.)

My family and I were to sleep upstairs in the farmhouse, which was already a fascinating experience, because it was an old-style European farm, with all facilities under one roof. It makes sense. When the farmer wants to check his horses or cows, he simply steps outside the kitchen door and there they are, mere feet away, essentially in the next room. (Odor, you ask? This guy's livestock was housebroken, so there was no odor other than the warm, pleasant smell of clean animals.) As the farmer showed us our room and the bathroom, he cautioned us against walking through one door that he pointed out to us in the hall. My curiosity got the best of me. "What's behind the door?" I asked.

Nodding, smiling, the farmer took us to the door and opened it. It was the chimney. All the fireplaces and stoves of the house emptied into one large, central brick chimney. This door opened directly into the chimney. And hanging there on iron poles, in constant smoke, were sausages, bacon, hams, roasts, pork chops, and hocks. Is that clever or what?!

But back to my cooking structures: in front of my old log cabin down in the river bottoms, there's a fire pit, a remnant of a time when a buddy showed up with a dead hog, and we roasted the whole thing in a pit full of coals and hot rocks for a couple days. When we dug out the hog, I just left the hole, and it became our campfire pit. I hauled in some big logs and put a couple planks across some concrete blocks around it by way of furniture. The best idea I had was driving a couple of old iron fence posts diagonally into the top of the back of the pit, sticking out over the fire. We hang coffeepots, kettles, and Dutch ovens—all sorts of things— from short pieces of chain hooked on the fence posts. Until I built my summer kitchen, I spent many quiet, happy hours sitting at that fire, cooking those pungent dishes men love and Linda won't let me cook in the house—*jaternice* (pronounced "ITH-ur-nit-see": a Czech sausage made of hogs' heads, heart, liver, and stale bread—the bread has to be stale, no kidding!), lutefisk (a Norwegian delicacy consisting of cod rendered inedible by soaking it in lye—again, no kidding!), and game foods (like beaver tail). No kidding.

Jaternice

    1 hog head, preferably scalded and cleaned but not
        skinned
    pork hocks, if you have them
    2 additional snouts, if you have them
    2 or 3 pork hearts
    3 pork or beef tongues (to be boiled separately until
        outer cover peels off and is then discarded)

one raw pork liver
Chunks of shoulder fat
2 loaves of day-old bread,
     maybe some pearled barley, if you can get it
4 cloves garlic
salt to taste
1 large onion
2–4 teaspoons pork seasoning
Casings

Cut meat into fist-size chunks and soak in cold water overnight. In the morning wash the meat, salt, and bring to a rolling boil for an hour. Debone and grind the meat in a grinder, but keep the meat warm. Soak bread in water, squeeze dry (no kidding!), and grind. Mash garlic in salt. Mix all ingredients together.*

Stuff into casings. Strain head stock, put in large kettle. Bring to a boil and cook sausages slowly, about 20 minutes. Rinse in cold water. Hang on rods to cool. To serve, fry slowly until brown. Best with lightly fried eggs.

I have prepared *jaternice* simply by boiling the materials together with a little extra of the head stock an extra half hour at where I inserted the asterisk [*] and then packing the result into plastic bags. I let the bags cool (I was cooking outside at the fire pit and it was snowing pretty good at the time, so it was easy enough to let it cool!) and put the bags in the freezer to be enjoyed at leisure.

Consider this recipe. To my mind, it is the ultimate peasant recipe. For example, there aren't any real proportions—a handful of this, some of that, hunks of those, one or two of these. It calls for the most inferior parts of the hog (in fact, the stuff most people—certainly rich people—would throw away! A pig's head, for God's sake!), stale bread, guts, livers, snouts, and ears. Jeez! Like most peasant food, it is also delicious. And like most peasant food, it is the kind of stuff that will keep a man working in the fields all day long without hunger.

If you're squeamish about recipes like the one above, consider that all the parts mentioned are only a few inches from the prime cuts the rich folks are eating up in the castle, and all under the same skin. My old man tells the story about the woman who comes into the butcher shop and says, "I want a cut of meat that is inexpensive, but I don't want to pay for a lot of bone or fat. I want something I can serve for supper tonight and then cut into sandwiches for my husband's lunch box tomorrow."

"I have just the thing for you." The butcher smiles. "Tongue!"

"Oh my my my!" the woman groans. "I don't want anything that came out of a filthy cow's mouth! Give me a dozen eggs!"

Let that be a lesson to you.

Lutefisk

Maybe you should think about this. A 100 percent, pure-blooded son of the Vikings once told me his forefathers wandered the world in their dragon boats, robbing, killing, and raping every step of the way mostly so they wouldn't have to go home to a supper of lutefisk. Not everyone loves lutefisk the way I do. Long ago I spent my Christmases in a very Norwegian family, and we had lutefisk every year. I remember the very first

time I tried the stuff. I walked into a house full of
Norwegians, steam, and a smell very much like
a cat food factory. Man. A lot of the
conversation among the relatives, I found,
centered on the impending supper and me. "I
wonder how many he'll eat," one said. "I remember
Ralph. First time, he didn't even eat one," said another.
"I'll bet he doesn't eat one whole one."

As it turned out, they weren't speculating on how
much I could eat because the main course was going to
be so good, but because they considered it so evil-
tasting. Why on earth would anyone ever serve food
they don't like, especially to guests, especially on the
auspicious occasion of a family gathering, particularly
on Christmas? Tradition, that's why. On Christmas, if
you're Norwegian, you eat lutefisk.

They didn't know me well. I loved the stuff. I was still
sitting there scarfing down lutefisk when the rest had
retreated from the table in disgust. Lutefisk is eaten as a
sort of Scandinavian burrito. You start with a large, thin,
potato pancake called a *lefsa*. You take some of the
gelatinous, stinking lutefisk from a bowl, dig out the ever-
present bones, put it on the lefsa, add some boiled
potatoes and butter, roll up the burrito, and eat it,
melted butter running down your forearms and dripping
from your elbows. Use some restraint. The temptation is
to put too much stuff into the fragile lefsa, resulting in a
lutefisk blowout. Not pretty. Makes my mouth water just
to think of it.

Problem is, lutefisk stinks to beat hell. No more
diplomatic way to say it. It is made by soaking cod in
lye water and drying it. Old-timers insist it's then
supposed to be leaned against the front of a grocery

store for a few weeks, where it can pick up additional seasoning from passing dogs. Then it is boiled pretty much a full day to get the lye out and reconstitute it from its planklike form to that of fishy Jell-O. It ain't pretty even at this stage.

In fact, one popular story tells of the two Norwegians talking on Main Street, and one points to the other's dog and says, "Your dog there must have worms, the way he's licking his butt." "Nah," the other replies. "He's just been eating lutefisk and he's trying to get the taste out of his mouth."

Obviously, that's only a joke and a long ways from the truth. No dog would eat lutefisk. When I cook the stuff—always when Linda is out of town for a day or so—I take a mess of it (and believe me, "mess" is the word) up to my pal Eric, who runs the tavern. He likes lutefisk, too. Once we ate our fill and I took the rest of it back to the farm to feed the dogs. I thought they might like it. They eat cow poop, for Pete's sake. I tossed the fish into the yard. The dogs sniffed at it, circled it, sniffed again, and then . . . then I got a new assessment of exactly where lutefisk stands on the gastronomic scale: they *rolled* in it.

Beaver Tail

I told you to think twice before you try lutefisk. If I were you, I wouldn't think at all about beaver tail. I kept reading about how early trappers and traders on the Plains savored beaver tail, and I thought, well, I'd like to try that sometime myself. When a friend of mine trapped a couple beaver, therefore, I asked him if I could have the tails, and he whacked them off for me. I cooked them just as I had read was the preferred method: I nailed them to a board and stood them before a hot fire, and things moved along exactly as they were supposed to. The skin cracked and peeled off, the meat steamed and dripped fat, and eventually it was clearly done. Eager with anticipation, I cut off a piece and munched down on it. Yuk. The stuff is perfectly dreadful. I have no idea why the trappers and traders thought it was good unless they were a hell of a lot hungrier than I've ever been. Phew.

Reminds me of Dad's recipe for carp: Scale and clean the carp. Nail it to a clean pine board. Stand the fish and board close to and facing a hot campfire. When the fish is crisp and brown, remove it from the fire and let it cool. Remove the fish from the board. Throw away the fish and eat the board.

_____

The point is, you can make food anywhere. I know men who like kitchens—you know, *real* kitchens—and there are women who excel over the campfire, but it is my impression, my experience, that men do best with summer kitchens, barbecue grills, patio meat burners, smokers, smokehouses, and campfires. So why not take advantage of those inherent graces and gifts?

There are philosophic dangers and intellectual traps here. Believe me, I know. I've chewed off my foot in several of them. I think, for example, of a meal at our Dannebrog home during which I was about as nervous as Linda. In this case, we weren't cooking for a master foodsman like Jim Harrison, but for some Pawnee guests, and our fear was not so much that our food wouldn't be up to snuff as that it would be inappropriate, that we might violate tribal, clan, or personal taboos. (Of which there are many. I'll tell you about some of them later.) The Pawnee quickly put us at ease, however.

Linda put together a superb meal—roast beef, as I recall—and at some point, as we looked out our kitchen window past our patio and my barbecue grill, through the summer kitchen to my smoker, the subject of my cooking came up. Linda joked about my standing banishment and our agreement that if I won't cook indoors, she won't cook outdoors, and I laughed that off by giving my usual lecture about how men are supposed to cook outside, over a fire, out where they can protect the family from saber-toothed tigers and, er, uh, dinosaurs.

"That's funny," Linda retorted. "You usually say you're protecting us from Indians."

"Oh, my God," said Vance Horse Chief, "and here they are!"

"And in our house!" added Robert Chapman.

"And at our table!" they all shouted in unison.

But the real clincher came when the meal was over and Linda remarked as, as usual, she started doing the dishes, "Where I was raised, those who do the cooking don't have to do the dishes."

I tossed in my usual line. "Where I grew up, we let the dogs clean the dishes."

To our surprise, Myron Echo Hawk jumped in, without a pause, with, "Where I grew up, we ate the dogs . . . didn't have no dishes!"

Now, that's real cooking, in my mind.

So, there you have it. Men cook outside, or as close to outside as they can get, because that's where they can keep their eye out for saber-toothed tigers. And Pawnee.

SOMEONE ELSE'S

Ultimately, the best place to eat is someone else's kitchen. Unfortunately, the worst place to eat is also someone else's kitchen. And the thing is, you never know. One thing for sure, never eat in some other guy's kitchen. Just assume right up front that he's no better a cook than you are. If he's cooked something real good, a specialty, something he's proud of, you'll hear about it from someone else, and chances are, when he's ready to share it, he'll bring it up to the tavern.

I don't know what the implications of that rule are for homosexuals. You know, it's more likely for a gay guy to be invited into a man's kitchen, don't you think? Not being a homosexual, I just don't know. I have nothing against homosexuals, and I know some good friends of mine are homosexuals, and I get along fine with them, but, as my bricklayer buddy Mick Maun says, I just don't want to know what they do for fun.

I also have intellectual problems with the idea of lesbians, but that's a little more complicated. Linda and I were once discussing the issue and my confusion—that I generally figure what people do consensually with one another is their own business, and most homosexuals and lesbians I know are nice folks, and most troublemakers—even sexual troublemakers—seem to be heteros, and while I have more of a grip—you should excuse the expression—on my problems with male homosexuals, I even have my problems dealing intellectually with lesbianism, and . . .

Then Linda jumped in and said, "Yes, it really is hard to imagine what it must be like to be a lesbian."

I nodded in agreement, and waited for her to elaborate.

She began to muse in a daydreamlike sort of way. "It

would be tough to come home to someone who's clean and smells good and doesn't need a shave."

I winced and was about to speak when she added, "And folds clothes out of the dryer, and leaves the toilet lid down."

I opened my mouth. "And can cook bean soup without destroying the kitchen and takes her shoes off when she comes in the door and can shop for groceries without coming home with two hundred dollars' worth of avocado dip and sunflower seeds and doesn't use a spatula to stir paint, and. . . ."

Fifteen or twenty minutes into this monologue, I muttered something about having to adjust the carburetor on a tractor, and drifted out to the shop. I'm still not sure where she was going with all that. Does that mean she doesn't understand homosexuals either?

Anyway, if you're a guy, and the other guy is, you know, like a guy guy, I recommend that you not jump at the chance of a free meal over at his place, since it might consist of Fritos and Bush's Beans out of the can, just like at your place, except you know who's been licking the spoons at your place. And I don't know anything about ladies, so I won't offer any advice there. The question then comes, What about when a woman invites you over to her place?

There is considerable risk here, and you might want to think about it. Harriett Nielsen runs the café here in town. She's maybe sixty-five years old and a widow, and I knew and loved her husband, Bumps, very much. And I know for a fact she can cook to beat hell. When she invites me in for snacks or breakfast or whatever, I'm in that door. But imagine that some gorgeous young woman invites you to her apartment for a very special meal, implying a very special evening, and you know she isn't talking about hors d'oeuvres. (This happened to me. This is not a hypothetical story.) You go up the long stairs to her austere but tasteful place. As you knock at the door, you hear soft, even romantical, music inside. She welcomes you with a gentle kiss on the cheek. She smells for all the world like heaven. She is gorgeous beyond belief. She is wearing an apron, *and to all appearances knows what she is doing in the kitchen*. "I bought some Jack Daniel's green label for you because I know you like it," she smiles. "Help yourself."

You take the bottle, splash a little JD-green in the glass she gives you, pretty much emptying the bottle, and you go to the refrigerator. You open the door and find . . . one slice of Velveeta Individual Pak cheese and a half-eaten container of raspberry yogurt. And that's it. Now think a moment: Is this what the refrigerator of a *cook* looks like?

You open the freezer door to get some ice and find . . . a glacier that would be quite at home in Greenland. There is no way to get out the ice cube tray, one of the old metal kind, with a little lever to loosen the cubes, because it is buried deep within, oh, maybe thirty or forty years' worth of blue ice. For all you know, the only thing in there is the frozen carcass of a prehistoric man.

That's okay. You can drink the whiskey neat. You sit at the kitchen table and watch this vision of beauty in an apron move through the process of preparing her special meal for you. "Now, where is that fork?" she says. "I know I have a fork here somewhere. While I'm looking, would you mind dusting the table, Rog?"

I won't bore you with how the meal went. And it's none of your business how the evening went after the meal. I did wind up marrying the woman, my beloved Lovely Linda, and it was no time at all before she became a masterful cook—no kidding. But I hope you sense the tension of this scenario. The question inevitably arises, "Will the rest of the evening"—if you get my drift—"suffer if she is poisoning me?" It may, as it was in my case, be a chance worth taking, but there is an alternative: Don't tempt the fates.

Bring your own food. Well, maybe not *your* food, but food you have somehow secured, maybe from Harriett. Or Chinese, or a picnic. That's always a good courting meal—a picnic. Not many dishes, lots of stuff you eat with your fingers (and boy, do I have a story for you later about that!), romantic notions, all that. I tried that with Linda, too—a breakfast picnic: bagels, lachs (a.k.a. lox), champagne, caviar, zwieback, French bread, Swiss chocolate. She liked the salmon and bagels but not the caviar, and got goofy over the chocolate and champagne.

I should perhaps also note that when I took up with Linda, as they say around here, she was sort of engaged to another guy. When she tossed her lot in with me, her former boyfriend threw at her, as his final indignation, "Do you actually think he's going to sit around and wait for you to learn how to cook?!" Yeah, I did, and every meal she cooks is a good one, and on the frequent occasion of a particularly great meal, I lift my glass in a toast of gratitude, and say, "Here's to you, Mikey—you dumb shit!"

These days, when I want to do something romantic, I call up our good friend Dee, who is a top-notch cook. I tell her roughly what I have in mind (by way of food), and she fixes it and brings it over. I pay her lavishly, which in our little town is still about twenty bucks. Then I do the dishes. Nothing charms a married woman like a man who'll do the dishes. Even if you're a bachelor and not very popular, you could do worse than once a week, or once a month, have a good cook you can fall back on to cook you a decent if not decadent meal and deliver it so you can think about what it would be like to be rich and married to a good cook.

HOLY DELICIOUS

If you insist on eating elsewhere, I still have some hints, but we are really on thin ice here. All too often there are bad surprises. Of course there are also some good surprises. My favorite good surprise was the time I was lecturing at Creighton University, in Omaha, and my host told me that she figured I might not want to go to some fancy restaurant and eat by myself (precisely, of course, what I would have preferred), so she had arranged for me to go eat with the Jesuit fathers at their quarters. Oh, great. That sounds like a lot of fun, supper with a pack of priests at their monastery, eating gruel and drinking warm water in absolute silence except for the Gregorian chants—and me not even being a Catholic.

That, of course, was the crux of the matter. I'm not a Catholic. So I didn't know what eating with Jesuits meant. The priest who walked me to the Jesuit House was dressed casually, and he seemed friendly enough, so I gritted my teeth and remembered that I would be picking up my honorarium later that evening. As we entered the Jesuit quarters, the priest asked, "Would you like a drink?"

"Sure," I said.

"What do you like?"

"Whiskey?" You're always safe with straight whiskey.

"What kind of whiskey?" They had a choice to offer?

"Well, let's cut to the chase: do you have a single-malt Scotch?"

"What kind of single-malt Scotch?"

Whew. They had maybe five different kinds of single

malts, and just about anything else that counts. They cooked their steaks right and we joked and laughed so hard that I was hoarse when it came time for me to give my evening lecture. What's the moral of the story? Well, I don't know what the moral is, except that sometimes meals from unlikely kitchens can come as pleasant surprises.

Jesuits

The Jesuits did their steaks right, as I have recommended above, but what's more, they served their whisky right (in case you're wondering about that spelling, American whiskey = whiskey; Scotch whisky = whisky). They served the whisky straight, maybe with the slightest splash of spring water (not tap water, whatever you do, if you get your water from a system where chlorine is used to purify it!!). One spring water ice cube is okay too, but please, don't make a single-malt Scotch tea or mix that nectar with anything but good, pure water!

Now for the important part, the jokes I can remember from the long evening of joke telling with the Jesuit fathers.

Jesuit joke #1: This guy comes up to a cab in New York and asks the cabbie, "You got room in there for a twelve-pack and a couple pizzas?"

"Sure," says the cabbie.

Joke teller opens an imaginary car door, leans forward, and barfs dramatically. Maybe it's funnier when a priest does it.

Jesuit joke #2: Saint Peter and Jesus are sitting around chatting at the Pearly Gates when they see an ancient, battered old man struggling up the long steps to Heaven. When he finally reaches the Gates, Jesus engages him in conversation: "Tough life, old man?"

"Very tough. I was poor, a worker with a child to raise."

"Oh, yes? What did you do for a living when you were on Earth?"

"I worked with wood, a carpenter of sorts."

"Hmmm," says Jesus, with growing curiosity. "And your child . . . was perhaps a son?"

"Well, yes," the old man muses, "but he wasn't exactly *my* son. In fact, he wasn't even exactly a human being."

Jesus steps forward with excitement. "Father?!!"

The old man looks up with light in his old eyes and cries, "Pinocchio?!!"

Church food can be terrific food, but only, I find, if it is meant for people who are not members of that particular church. Members of churches generally seem to think that they can best impress fellow parishioners by demonstrating the humility, poverty, and suffering they suffer when they eat at home. Church dinners meant for outsiders, on the other hand, are almost always wonderful devices for converting the heathen; the message is, "See how God feeds his chosen?"

I recall a duck and sauerkraut dinner I once attended with my wife's family in some tiny Czech town in eastern Nebraska. The meal was advertised as "Duck, kraut, and all the fixings, including homemade pie," for which they nailed us something like six dollars.

Well, we went through the line and got generous helpings of roast duck, potatoes, dressing, gravy, creamed corn, homemade bread, and . . . and . . . no pie. I was disappointed, but considering the generosity of the servers with everything else, I wasn't about to complain, so I went docilely to my place at the long table of scarfers. And then a lady came by with our pie—one for every four diners. Um-um, and was it good!

Similarly, two friends and I once went to a church dinner in the Mexican community of Scottsbluff, Nebraska. We went through the line and ate, not saying a lot. Not because there was nothing to say but because the food was so incredibly good that no one wanted to waste time talking. We finished the wonderful food, sat there grinning and sighing, looked at one another, and instantly, unanimously, simultaneously came to the same conclusion: We needed to go through that line again. And we did. And we were so totally bloated, we couldn't get into the car to leave—so we walked home. The double meals cost each of us twelve dollars. If they had been serving the next day, we would have gone back again. For breakfast, if we could have.

FOREIGN AGAIN

My favorite ethnic eateries are places that don't advertise they are ethnic. Tony's Diner in Cairo, Nebraska, says nothing about being Greek, but is it ever Greek, and in an area where there are few Greeks otherwise. (I once asked Sophie, the proprietor of Tony's, how she came to be in Nebraska, and she explained perfectly, poetically, "This GI, he come to Europe to serve his country. He see this gorgeous Grik girl. He is enchanted, he is in love . . . and here I am!!") How about Dino's Diner in Columbus, Nebraska? It's Chinese, and damned good Chinese. So, who's Dino? Look for places like that, and when you find one, tell everyone about it, so it will stay in business.

I wish I could help you judge where the good restaurant food is, but I've never figured it out for myself. People have told me never to eat at a place called Mom's or where home cooking is advertised, and that generally seems like good advice. I haven't had good luck with places that have themes or tack antique crap on the walls. But there are always exceptions. The best Oriental restaurant in Nebraska—maybe America—is in Grand Island: Yen Ching's. Yen Ching's breaks all the rules: it has Chinesey decor, its waitresses wear Orientalish outfits, and it is popular even with the local businessmen for lunch. The bottom line is that the food is superb, every time, every day. William Least Heat Moon, a friend of mine, uses his calendar index (the more calendars hanging on the wall, the better the food) to judge restaurants. The notion about picking a place with a lot of trucks in the parking lot sure as hell doesn't carry much water these days. I just don't catch many clues to offer you.

Perhaps most important is to follow your instincts and always pick peasant food. Look at it this way: aristocrats eat mostly to impress other people; peasants eat to eat. When I was a little kid, Mom worked as a domestic for some rich folks in Lincoln. She cooked, served, that sort of thing, for big, fancy, opulent parties. And on weekends when she was working the rich folks, I stayed up waiting for her to come home.

The people she worked for were really very nice folks, and they would often send her home with a box of leftovers, as often as not the canapés that wouldn't be much use to the household the next week anyway. So here we were, lower-class German factory workers, and Mom came home with caviar, lachs, pâté, all the rich-folks stuff. Not a lot of it, but enough so I got a chance to sample it, and to remember it well into my maturity.

On the other hand, Mom never took samples of our food—*runzas, Schnitzsupp', rivelkuche, grebel*—for the rich folks to sample. So who wound up with the widest culinary experience in that exchange? Obviously, the peasants. And that's the way it's been for millennia, believe me. So when it comes to knowing what the hell food is all about, it's the poor people you can count on.

In England, therefore, don't go to some fancy three-star restaurant, because you are going to be disappointed, I guarantee you. Walk into some small-town pub and order a shepherd's pie or ploughman's lunch or bubble and squeak. And a pint of local bitter. And some cheese from the farmer up the road. And some of that bread the barkeep is eating. Ah, it makes my mouth water just to think of it.

Actually, I learned this little strategy from one of America's truly great food experts, Dr. Jay Anderson, of Utah State University, in Logan. I've traveled with him in about twenty countries of the world, and it has been some of my best traveling. If you like a tidy automobile, don't travel with Jay Anderson. You just start dozing off when suddenly the car slams to a stop, pops into reverse, and the car careens fifty yards backward into a ragged farmyard somewhere in Wales. "Look at that!" he yells, pointing at a dim sign written on a board, maybe thirty years ago, and tacked on the side of a stone farmhouse. "Brfflmngmststqq [They speak Welsh in Wales and that's what Welsh looks like, believe me] cheese for sale."

Before you can say anything, Jay has engaged some old gent in conversation, charmed his wife out of two pounds of incredible cheese for fifty cents, and followed the voluptuous young hired girl to an outbuilding, where there is allegedly some homebrew beer and fresh bread.

This goes on day after day for weeks when you travel with Jay. Pretty soon the car is full of the remnants of cheese wheels, breads so good you can't bear to throw away the two-pound heels that are left over, various sausages made out of potatoes or blood or thistles or whatever that particular peasant makes his sausage out of, and maybe forty half-full bottles. Thing is, when Jay buys beer or wine or whiskey, it's always a scientific experiment, so you have to buy two bottles of each kind the seller happens to have in stock or in his basement or back in her apartment. (You laugh!) You can't drink it all, but then you can't throw it away either, because you'll almost certainly want to compare it with the eighteen bottles of whatever you buy tomorrow. Or later this evening. Or around the next bend in the road.

I cannot possibly recall all the times I've sat in a garden, on a porch, on a balcony, overlooking some gloriously bucolic scene, enjoying something remarkable—Cuban cigars, Dutch chocolate, Finnish vodka, Swedish beer, German sausage, French cheese—thinking, "I wonder what the rich folks are eating."

A CINDERELLA STORY

My favorite Jay Anderson story is memorable for a number of reasons, each valid, each one alone worthy of remembering. Jay and I were working at the Plimoth Plantation Museum in Plymouth, Massachusetts. Jay was working with the museum and its director, Jim Deetz, investigating the foods the Pilgrims ate. There were a lot of surprises. The Pilgrims ate with their fingers mostly, for example, and weren't at all crazy about this maize stuff.

And, my favorite surprise, the Pilgrims were hopeless

lushes. Yep, John Alden, Priscilla, Bradford, the whole crowd. A woman brewed a barrel of beer for her family of ten or twelve about once a week, meaning each and every man, woman, and child drank maybe a half case of young beer each and every day. That beer was a little lower in alcohol content than ours (but not far from one of our current, reprehensible light beers), but a half case is a lot of suds.

I had some advanced training in the history and chemistry of fermentation, and I was at the Plymouth museum to help malt barley and turn it into our best guess at what the Pilgrims drank. It was March, cold and snowy, and we were staying in one of the Pilgrim houses. Malting is a constant and delicate process, so we had to stay with our work night and day. We were cold and not at all comfortable, but then neither were the Pilgrims, so . . .

One evening, Jay and I were sitting huddled in front of our miserable fire, watching our fermenting beer bubbling in the barrel, wrapped in blankets, and understanding better and better every hour why so many Pilgrims called it quits and went home or killed themselves. One of the curators, a lovely, bosomy, thoroughly healthy woman with a lilting English accent, dropped by to see how we were doing. We were doing better. She took off her shoes and tucked her legs under her as she sat with us on the only bed in the room, which, lit only by flashes from the fire on the hearth, was suddenly warmer.

After a brief conversation, Jay said, "Rog, maybe this is the time to break out that special dessert we brought." He nodded toward a chest where we had stashed a bottle of Glencoe single-malt Scotch whisky, 104 proof, the only bottle of that nectar I have seen in my entire sixty years of life despite an endless search. I threw open the chest and pulled out the bottle. We broke the seal and poured a generous dram into some plastic cups we had also sneaked into this environment where everything was supposed to be strictly as it was in 1627. Wow. In the firelight the whisky glowed. And it was delicious.

Then something extraordinary happened. Our visitor set her whisky on the edge of the bed so she could get more comfortable (gasp choke). The wretched bed was unsteady to begin with, and with three of us sitting on it, her movement caused just enough of a tremor to send the full glass of that glorious drink off the edge. Jay and I both lurched toward it, but we were way too slow to rescue it. It fell, upside down, precisely and totally, into her shoe. Jay's hesitation was so brief, I admire it to this moment. It was not so much a matter of doubt as it was of timing. He picked up her shoe, lifted it to us as if in a toast, and downed the whisky therein. And you wonder why I admire Jay Anderson. He should run tours with buses that lurch through the countryside of countries, any countries, stopping wherever and whenever, eating, drinking, filling the bus with the rubble of meals seized at whatever opportunities presented themselves.

I once ate at a four-star restaurant with Jay. It was okay.

FANCY IS WHAT FANCY ISN'T

I was in Monterrey, Mexico, one January, exercising some defiance, sitting in the January sun on a hotel balcony, sipping some incredibly cheap but remarkably good tequila, when I decided to treat myself to a meal at the best place in all of Monterrey, whatever that might be. I asked around a little, and there was a consensus: the best restaurant in all of Monterrey was La Rosa. So I went there. The meal was, at best, mediocre. A strolling string band in Zorro outfits annoyed diners at enormous cost and the waiters were inattentive, but that was okay, because I sure as hell didn't want any more of that kind of food, anyway.

The next day I noticed that a family had set up a kind of fast-food operation in the old cloakroom of the modest hotel where I was staying. They were cooking over a small stove and handing out food on newspapers to other workers in the area. I watched them a few seconds, and my instincts told me to give it a try the next evening. I talked with them about my plans . . . well, not really talked, since I know no Spanish and the only English between us was through a six- or seven-year-old boy who had studied some of the language in school. I explained that I wanted a full sampling of local fare, plenty of it; I'd spring for a plate and cup; and I wanted to eat it in the patio area of the hotel. They probably thought I was a little goofy, but they went along with the gringo.

The food was terrific. I mean *terrific*. It was so good, the memory of it brings tears to my eyes. When I staggered back and paid my piddly bill for the meal, I tried as best I could to explain to the young English student of the family that I had eaten at La Rosa the night before, but the food his family was serving here in the hotel was definitely superior. The kid finally showed a sign of understanding, and ran into the back room. I heard a flurry of excited Spanish and the punctuation of "LA ROSA!!!" followed by a family cheer.

I ate with those folks every night the rest of the time I was in Monterrey.

When it comes to food, reputation ain't nothin', folks. Nothin'.

HOME COOKIN'

One more story along that line: when I was a mere stripling of a lad, I had a fraternity brother who was raised on a

Nebraska farm by his Swedish parents. I thought the food that came from the fraternity house kitchen was pretty good, considering. In fact, he and I were both in the Nebraska Air National Guard, too, and I thought the food there was pretty good. Considering.

What it lacked in epicurean finish, it made up for in metric tonnage: there was always *lots* of food, especially milk . . . chocolate milk, buttermilk, all I could drink—and I could drink a lot. I cost the government a fortune during those years, and took hundreds of American dairy farmers through some tough economic times.

Bob didn't like the food. He complained bitterly . . . *bitterly!* He was damn near disabled by his yearnings for the wonders and delicacies, the substance and subtlety, of his Swedish mother's rural kitchen and cupboard. And I sympathized with him. My heart ached for him. I mean, jeez, my mom is a terrific cook, but she isn't Swedish, and she didn't have access to all that fresh farm butter and eggs and beef and home-cured bacon and fresh produce and, well, all those things. I still ate the fraternity and National Guard food, but I couldn't take my eyes off Bob's sorrowful face.

Then Bob invited me to come visit his family for the weekend, and my heart—or maybe it was my stomach—rejoiced. We left very early on a Saturday morning so we could get to the farm in time for breakfast. It was still dark when we hit the highway; the sun was only coming over the horizon as we drove into the farmyard two hours later. We blustered into the kitchen and were at once smacked in the face by a mess of powerful, not altogether pleasant smells. His mother was all I expected—a fat little lady with a round, sweaty face, even though it was almost winter outside, dressed in an apron, a swirl of steam around her brow. Oh man, is this going to be great or what?!

Well, the coffee left something to be desired—it was weak and a little off flavor, as if it had been boiled or maybe was a day or two old—but the eggs and sausage . . . well, the eggs were runny and had bits of shell in them, and the sausage was overseasoned and was, as I recall, Jimmy Dean stuff out of a plastic bag. The toast was burned, and the jelly was cheap stuff from a grocery store jar. The juice was Tang! The bacon was undercooked, the silverware was dirty, there were cats everywhere, and Bob's mother was about as friendly as Roseanne Barr.

After the leaden biscuits had been washed down with bluish, wangy milk, Bob leaned back in his chair, patted his stomach, smiled at me, and said, "Now, that's eating, ain't it?" I think I said something about it sure not being what we got at the fraternity. I made it through the next two days, but what I learned was not so much gustatory as anthropological: Every man's mother is a great cook.

BAR NONE

The one last offering I have for the gentleman dining in a kitchen not his own is the local tavern. When Linda goes off somewhere for a few days, she acts as if I'm going to die of malnutrition. There are things a man does to keep his woman happy, and one of them is to go along with the fiction that he is helpless without her. (Hint: if there is a woman in your life and she goes away for a few days, try to keep the place basically decent. I do this by abandoning the house and sleeping on the back porch until the morning of her return. But—and this is important!—leave some sort of mess for her to discover and clean up. I am fond of leaving a few dishes in the sink, socks on the living room floor, coffee stains on the kitchen floor, or—my personal favorite—evidence of a small explosion in the microwave. This will give her the opportunity on her return to click her tongue a few times and clean up the "mess," remarking about how helpless men are without a woman in the house, while you stand with your head hanging on your chest, saying, "And gosh, dear, am I ever hungry. Haven't had a bite to eat since Tuesday.")

Of course, men know cheesy popcorn has most of the nutrients known necessary to the male metabolism when mixed liberally with beer and pickled eggs. When I make my table at Eric's Tavern up in town, I start with an aperitif of cold Budweiser with a handful of stale Brazil nuts from his gourmet nuts selection. A Bloody Mary with plenty of celery salt (some places even serve a Bloody Mary with a celery stick for a stirrer, a nutritional plus if there ever was one!) fulfills the metabolism's need for vegetable fiber.

For a main course, I usually select a large bag of pork rinds and maybe a length or two of hot sausages. All washed down with a few more mugs of cold beer, of course. For dessert, a candy bar and a few more beers will satisfy even the most demanding palate. Now, there are almost certainly going to be some hoity-toity nutritionists who will do what they can to make a fuss about how some vitamin or another is missing from that diet, but in the long run, it's all there.

And if it isn't, chomp on a few of Uncle Roger's Nutritional Bombshells and everything will be fine again.

Uncle Roger's Nutritional Bombshells

This is an absolute invention of my own. You've never heard of this one anywhere else. I discovered it by accident once when I was inventorying the contents of my refrigerator and found I had only one thing: a jar of Vlasic's Mild Greek Pepperoncini green peppers.

And in the cupboard I had only one other thing—a bag of English walnut halves. I ate them together—a pepper into my mouth, a nut into my mouth. And they were delicious. The peppers are good and the walnuts are good but together they become something entirely different. It's like adding two and two and getting six. Try it and see if I'm not right.

Real-man cooking leads to discoveries like my nutritional bombshells. Cooking by recipe doesn't. Who would guess that a peanut-butter-and-bacon sandwich is so good it will bring tears to your eyes? It does. Add lettuce, and you have a complete meal, with every known daily nutrient needed by the average 200-pound man.

Want to have some fun? The next time you eat a bag of pork rinds, take a look at the nutritional stats on the back of the bag. Isn't that amazing? Zero vitamin A, zero vitamin B, zero vitamin C, zero iron, zero calcium, zero nutrients, "not a significant source of protein," it says right on the sack—nothing else useful—but 250 fat calories (half your daily fat allowance all told), 70 percent of your day's sodium, lots of salt, fat, and twelve-syllable preservative chemicals. It's gotta be good for you. Or your cardiologist, one or the other.

VITTLES

That which Pythagoras said to his scholars of old, may be forever applied to melancholy men, *A fabis abstinete*, eat no beans.

> —ROBERT BURTON,
> *The Anatomy of Melancholy,*
> *Democritus to the Reader,* 1621

Eat no onions or garlick for we are to utter sweet breath.

> —SHAKESPEARE,
> *A Midsummer Night's Dream,* 1595

Five breakfast burritos—extra beans, extra onions, extra cheese, extra whatever else you got in there.

> —DENNIS "LUNCHBOX" ADAMS,
> McDONALD'S DRIVE-THROUGH
> WINDOW, YORK, NEBRASKA, 1994

Embrace winter with pork products; lard is the fuel of conquest.

> —JIM HARRISON,
> PRIVATE COMMUNICATION, 1995

WHAT'S FOR SUPPER?

Okay, we've settled on where we're going to do our cooking and eating, not necessarily in that order, so now we can start thinking seriously about man food itself. Again, let me head off some trouble by stressing once more that I am not saying there are things only men eat, or only men can eat, or only men should eat; nor am I suggesting there are things women eat, only women can eat, or only women should eat. Most men eat what most women eat. But it's my impression that, given a choice of whatever they want, men and women are not likely to choose consistently the same things to eat. Besides, it's my book, and I can say what I want to.

In my mind, food has two functions: nutrition and ceremony. Frankly, we can pretty much forget about nutrition. No one eats what's good for him. No one eats what

1. tastes best
2. is economical
3. is convenient
4. is most nourishing
5. makes sense ecologically

We eat things that make a statement about

1. wealth
2. politics
3. egos
4. fashion
5. sex
6. culture

Think about a meal that is composed only of things that make sense on the cash register tape, composed of foods in season and locally grown, full of vitamins and fiber and all that other stuff that's good for you, and causes the least possible damage to the environment. Doesn't leave much, does it? Nothing good, for sure.

Forget about the "tastes best" thing. You don't know what tastes best, because you haven't tried everything else, and what you're used to tastes good and what you're not used to probably doesn't, especially if it involves snakes or something called smut, which grows, incidentally, on corn kernels, and looks a little like a grain of corn except it is huge, bloated, lumpy, blue, globular, gross, and delicious. Just like truffles, a black fungus that grows underground, is rooted out by pigs, and costs a hundred dollars per teaspoonful.

Actually, we go out of our way to eat things that do *not* speak to the virtues above. Damn the environment, we seem to be saying. We want the best possible beef. I do, anyway. Convenient? How, by all that's practical, are coconut, French wine, and avocados convenient? Orange juice in Minnesota, swordfish in Nebraska, prime rib in Maine, and so it goes. Oh, there are plenty of apologists: "I eat all those things for a balanced diet, to make sure I have all the vitamins and other good things my body—which is a temple, after all—needs." So, I say, take a vitamin pill and save all the logistics. Nah. We like the stuff because we like the stuff.

And because there's stuff we don't like. Between Anita Bryant and Rush Limbaugh (a terrible between to contemplate, if you ask me), I don't care if I never drink another glass of orange juice—if that's what it is by the time it's been deconstituted, reconstituted, stabilized, preservatived, and boxed.

Actually, what we don't eat is about as interesting as what we do eat. My Jewish friend Izzy, for example, won't eat pork because of his religion. Unless there's nothing except the pork. Or nothing better than the pork. Or bacon hamburgers, which is somehow a different deal in his mind. As he explained it once, bacon is okay because you kind of scrape it off the outside of the pig's main construction, whereas pork chops, which Iz happens not to like all that much anyway, are from deep down inside that porker.

When I was a lad, it was always a coup to date a Catholic girl on a Friday, maybe for a football game, because then when you took them across town to King's Hamburger Castle, they would order a cheapie fish sandwich or cheese Frenchee. But you had to get them out of the place before midnight, or whammo, double cheeseburger with mushrooms and bacon and whatever else became magically and suddenly uncursed at the twelfth stroke of the clock.

My dad wouldn't let me date Catholic girls, however. He said I'd never have to worry about marrying one if I didn't date one. I dated only one. I married her. Somewhere along the line, for reasons I've never grasped (being theologically challenged), hamburgers had the curse lifted from them Friday-wise while I was still married to a Protestant girl (big mistake), but my Catholic bride still serves salmon patties, creamed peas, and macaroni and cheese on Fridays. I've tried to make the case that I bet the Pope doesn't eat salmon patties, cream peas, and macaroni and cheese on Fridays, without noticeable effect.

I am a member of the Wind Clan (cut the wisecracks, thank you) of the Omaha Indian tribe, and there are certain taboos that go along with that distinction; for example, I am not supposed to wear blue-green face paint, which is fairly easy to deal with, and no one is supposed to blow on me for fear of stirring up a tornado, but since tickling is okay, I haven't found that prohibition a burden, either. The tough part has been that I can't eat shellfish. No shrimp, lobster, clams, oysters, mussels, that sort of thing. That has been tough, because, before my adoption into the tribe, I loved those things a lot.

When I asked my Omaha brother what the nature of those prohibitions is ... like the meat on Friday for Catholic girls, or pork for Izzy, or maybe something one sacrifices for Lent ... he had to give it some thought. Then he said, "It's like putting your hand in the fire." What he meant is that there are substantial consequences. Even if you put your hand in a fire to rescue a baby, or you fall in accidentally, or you're blind and don't see the fire ... you will suffer the consequences of touching the fire.

I stewed on that a while myself, especially when I was on an airplane (gulp) and found that I had inadvertently scarfed down half a lobster omelet. (For those of you who are younger than forty, there was a time when they actually served real meals with actual food on airplanes, and sometimes it was really good. Nowadays we're too advanced to fuss with such nonsense.) I was pretty worried, up in that airplane, being a member of the Wind Clan who just ingested shellfish, I can tell you, but we landed safely, and I went about my work, consulting for a museum outside Philadelphia.

So far, so good. I didn't get sick. In fact, that evening I had a terrific time with some old friends, and we ate like pigs. I pretty much forgot the Omahas, the Wind Clan's food taboo thing, and thought along the lines "I am pure of heart, and therefore this time I walked through the fire without damage. Or maybe the old taboos no longer work. Or maybe because I am only a white man who has been converted into an Omaha. ... " At any rate, it seemed I had been spared the wrath of the Thunderers.

The next morning my friend and I returned to the museum to continue our work. At least to what was left of the museum. Everyone was standing around in complete bafflement, because a tornado had come right up the valley we were supposed to work in that day and had pretty much destroyed everything. This wasn't Kansas. This was Pennsylvania. They said they'd never heard of tornadoes in this part of the country. What could possibly have brought about this strange turn of meteorological events? they wondered. I didn't say anything, but I've been damned careful about eating shellfish since then, I can tell you.

I also can't drink milk anymore—some kind of lactose intolerance. Anything with milk or cream and I'm at the edge of a gastric Mt. Saint Helens, just like that. There is a new study from some scientific smarty-pants saying that no one is really lactose intolerant and that anyone can drink a glass or two of milk without effect. I challenge this bonehead to lock himself in a closet with me for two hours after I drink a glass of milk. There'd be one scientist with a new sense of empirical evidence, that's for sure.

To carry this whole digression one more step (and then I promise I'll stop), how about those things some people are not supposed to eat but do anyway, all the while insisting they don't? The standard joke around my little town of 322 people is that the biggest difference between the Lutherans and Baptists is that the Baptists buy their alcohol in Grand Island . . . where they can't be seen. A story to that issue tells of the town picnic, where some rascals cut plugs into some of the watermelons and filled them with grain alcohol. Later that afternoon, someone noticed that the Catholic priest was eating watermelon just as fast as he could. The Lutheran minister was caught lugging a couple extra melons to his car before he left. And the Baptist preacher was crawling around on his hands and knees collecting seeds.

My cousin Wayne wouldn't eat onions when he was a kid. Maybe he still won't—I'll have to ask him. Anyway, when he was a kid, he wouldn't eat onions. He was staying over with us on one occasion or another when Mom and Aunt O'Linda were gone somewhere, leaving my dad to take care of us. And do the cooking. As far as I know, and I've known him a long time, Dad cooks only two things: steaks on the grill and fried potatoes. His fried potatoes are good but pretty basic: mostly just fried potatoes, sometimes with hamburger or sausage—and onions. Well, Pop stirred up a mess of spuds for us and dumped a load on each of our plates. Wayne took one look and announced, "I don't eat onions."

"Well," said Dad without hesitation, "I can understand that, because I don't eat onions, either." I looked on with substantial surprise. Huh? No onions?

"But there are onions in here," Wayne protested.

"Nope, no onions," said Dad, digging in with enthusiasm.

"What are these, then, if they're not onions?"

"That, my boy, is Rooshen fried cabbage."

Us being "Rooshens" and all—German colonists from the Volga valley of Russia, actually—Wayne pretty much had to accept that these things that look for all the world like onions were actually part of our heritage, our soul food, if you will—kraut for Krauts. So Cousin Wayne ate a plate's worth.

"Yep," said Dad, "Rooshen fried cabbage is to us Rooshens pretty much what spinach is to Popeye."

And Cousin Wayne ate another plateful. I don't know if he still eats Rooshen fried cabbage. I'll have to ask him sometime.

Rooshen Fried Cabbage

Most of my life I have been a field worker in folklore—traditional materials. And one of my specialties was ethnogastronomy—traditional foodways. At first it was frustrating to try to collect "recipes" from traditional cooks; then it got to be funny. For one thing, real cooks don't use recipes. They know their kitchen and things like ingredients like a classical pianist knows the piano. They go by feel and look and common sense and intuition and a sense of adventure. So when I asked someone for a recipe, I got a blank look more often than not. "Recipe? There's no recipe! You just make it the way it's always made."

Just for fun, however, I asked Dad for his recipe for Rooshen Fried Cabbage, knowing full well what I was going to get. He didn't disappoint me. Here is what he wrote me:

"Peel potatoes. Cut in thin, round pieces. Put a little lard in frying pan. Put potatoes, onions, and a little salt and pepper in frying pan. Put lid on pan. Light burner on stove. Put pan on burner. Stir occasionally until potatoes turn light brown."

And there you are. Any questions? Just make 'em the way the way they're always made.

FOOD TO FILL THE HEART

But I digress. This started off with my saying something about there being two functions for food, nutrition and cere-mony. So it follows that there are two kinds of food you need to consider: food to fill your belly and food to fill your heart. You're not going to believe what I'm about to say next, but here it goes anyway. Women are drawn to food for nutrition—they are the caretakers, they want to see everyone stuffed, everyone loaded with vitamins and proteins and things to make the body healthy.

That makes sense, right? Most of you find that easy enough to accept. Its corollary is a little more difficult to swallow: therefore, men are drawn to the ceremonial elements of food. Yeah, yeah, I know. We think of men as choking down whatever the hell is on the table, whatever they can grab on the way through the cash counter at the local Stop and Gas, 7-Come-11, or Choke and Puke. Jeez, men go hunting, sit in a cold, wet duck blind for days at a time, sit there cuddled up with wet dogs, everyone smelling pretty much the same after a couple hours, sharing fleas as much as food, knock down a duck, cut it up right on the spot, toss it in a frying pan warmed over a camp stove reeking of gas, and choke the half-raw bird between shots at ducks and out of a bottle. That's ceremony?

Yes, it is. What the hell are they doing out there in the first place? Putting food on the table? Puh-leez! They could save a couple thousand dollars a year if they bought the finest cuts of beef in the grocery store instead of going hunting. They are there for a reason, and it isn't comfort, economy, taste, convenience, all those things I listed above. Ask them what they're doing out there in the cold and rain. They'll give you a bunch of thoroughly goofy answers that make no sense at all—saving wildlife (oh yeah!), loving nature (by killing it? Get serious), putting food on the family table (!!!), but the fundamentals of what they're doing is killing. And there's something primal about that. And they are in the company of men doing men things. There's something primal about that, too. And they are eating men food.

What these guys are doing is fulfilling ritual duties just as surely as if they had painted up their bodies and put on peculiar, spirit-satisfying costumes (which they're sort of doing, if you think about it), and making incantations and sacrifices to the gods. And if you ask them what the food in the blind is like, the answer is almost certain to be that it is superb. Couldn't be better. Sort of like burnt sacrifices on the alters of the mystic powers, you know?

Mick's Blind Duck

Mick the Brick Maun's pride in his cookery is couched in the confidence that only he can cook it to perfection. He knows that since it has to be prepared on a freezing morning in a wet, stinking duck blind on a frozen lake in the company of a wet black dog who pants with such enthusiasm that his tongue flicks spit wildly about the tiny, cramped blind—so that anything that isn't wet from the lake or the dog, when he shakes off, or Gary, when he dried off the last time he fell backward into the lake, gets wet from the dog's spit flicking—no one else will ever duplicate *his* Blind Duck. Mick knows that the following recipe, when cooked in a kitchen, even a summer kitchen, or over a campfire, will never be right *because the conditions will never be right.* So he wrote it down for me.

The opening is revealing:

"The one thing about this taste-bud delight is that the duck has to be fresh-shot and only tastes proper in the duck blind. I think it has to do with the whaff of gun powder on a cold, still morn at the marsh."

I urge you, however, not to give up on the notion of trying out Mick's recipe for Blind Duck. I used to insist

that my Dutch oven–baked beans could never
taste the same in domesticity as they do in camp.
But I found that one can duplicate the experience
by spreading a five-gallon bucket of fine sand on
the kitchen floor, using cast-iron ware that was
not carefully cleaned the night before, when it was used
to fry fish in beer (since someone forgot the cooking oil),
sprinkling just a touch of wood ash from the fireplace
into the pot, drinking about a half quart of Jack Daniel's
green label before eating, and insisting that your guests
not bathe for three or four days before your dinner
party. It isn't exactly the same, but it comes close.

I suspect that one could do the same with Mick's
recipe. Drop the temperature in your house to about
25°, which will cause the pipes to freeze and burst, so
you and your guests will be suitably soaked and cold.
Be sure you ask your guests to bring their dogs. Eat in
the bathroom or, if you want to duplicate even more
closely the ambience of the duck blind, in the bathtub.
Pry open the top of six or seven shotgun shells and pour
out the shot. Be sure all the shot is removed, or you may
come closer to actual hunting conditions than you want.
Place the shells in a shotgun and fire them off in the
bathroom. Of course you'll be deaf and won't be able
to see across the bathtub for the smoke, but that's part of
the context for this recipe. Cook over a Coleman stove
because the odor of burning Coleman fuel adds a
certain je ne sais quoi to the dish. Ride a child's merry-
go-round until you feel queasy enough to duplicate the
feeling you get from sitting in a small boat for hours. Do
not season, because no one ever remembers the salt
and pepper; that's why Mick says below, "with
whatever spices you have." Eat the duck half raw

because the smell of the bacon will have made you hungry enough halfway into the cooking that there's no way in hell you can wait. Check with the dog. If he won't eat it, maybe you should send out for pizza.

But I'm being cruel. Mick is proud of his recipe and he generously shared it with me, so the least I can do is pass it along to you just as he sent it to me. And here it is.

"You want to start of course with that fresh-shot duck—one of the more exotic-tasting webfoots of the central flyway such as redheads, meaty and yummy-in-the-tummy!! (Blind tip #1: just 'cuz you're gonna eat this one doesn't mean you get to shoot one more. Be honest, duckers!) Take that fresh-shot (did I say fresh-shot before? Very important!) duck, strip the breast flesh, and filet that little rascal. Then cut into cubes like when they fon-doo in them fancy Oriental cafés. By now your bacon should be just about smoking in your cast-iron skillet. (Blind tip #2: Skillets should be well seasoned and scraped, not washed.)

"Remove crunchy bacon and throw in duck with whatever spices you have. We prefer garlic 'cuz it goes with everything, ice cream to steaks. (Blind tip #3: When ducking with retrievers, never set up the blind kitchen between said retriever and the exit—again very important.) Cook that cubed duck on the Coleman with heat set high enough to make it sizzle. When you can poke it with a fork and it doesn't bleed, it's ready to eat.

"This recipe is only meant as a whore dove, but it is great when you add potatoes O'Brian and eggs for a breakfast sensation you'll never see at Village Inn." [Author's note: For an explanation of "breakfast sensation," see "Boom John's Huevos Rancheros," and give a little thought to what it means to be out in a boat in the middle of an icy lake when the nearest outhouse, yet alone toilet, is maybe an hour and a quarter away. Not pretty, is it? That's why they chain the dog. And by the way, "whore dove" is Nebraskan for hors d'oeuvres.]

I submit that the positive qualities of food come from the comfort it gives to the heart, not the belly. Ask most women what they think of the cuisine in a duck blind, and they'll let you know in no uncertain terms.

Whatever a man's inclinations, however, he still must put together foods to keep the body together as well as the soul. But don't get me wrong: I'm no Freud. I still think even the simplest, most basic, most casual, fastest foods are a lot more than food. And often, what seems to be absolutely nothing but food winds up being a lot more. I'm not just talking about making good food better, although that certainly is a thought worth keeping. I like salads. What's a salad? A little lettuce, maybe some cress, a little dressing, an olive. But for me, a pretty ordinary salad can be made elegant with the addition of a teaspoon of capers (pickled tree buds, believe it or not) and a brace of anchovies, the fishiest of the fishy. I know, that's not everyone's idea of elegant, but it is for me. So my refrigerator is never without a little jar of capers and a tin of anchovies. It is a very small, very insignificant, very inexpensive way to make my life happier.

I offer that as an example of making decent food better, but in all honesty, I can't be sure that's the whole story. I have had some wonderful meals at a place called the Steak House, in Lincoln, Nebraska, and for years their salads were graced with . . . anchovies and capers. That's where I first learned about these morsels, forty years ago. So, do I like anchovies and capers because they're good, or because they conjure up all sorts of good memories? Does it matter? I like anchovies and capers, that's what counts.

Remember my story about making hams? Obviously, to me the whole matrix of curing those hams, hauling them down to the smokehouse, day after day keeping that smudge fire going, and then the joyous day of delivering those little bundles of joy from Christmas house to Christmas house is a lot more to me than just putting another hunk of meat in the freezer. It's my version of sitting in a duck blind, I guess. I was going to write in this paragraph that, hey, look, that whole ham thing started as nothing more than food but it became more. But it didn't even start just as food. It started as an educational demonstration for my children. I'm telling you, once you start thinking about it, you can't remember the last time you ate just because you were hungry. And I'll bet that if you told me the last time you ate because you were hungry, it wouldn't take long for me to figure out something else that was going on.

GETTING IT RIGHT

Even fast food can have its meaning. When we were teaching colleagues, Vic Lane and I used to take our lunches together at a drive-in food place in Lincoln, Nebraska, called the Tastee Inn. There's no other way to say it: The food was dreadful. The onion chips were greasy, the malts were tasteless, and a Tastee sandwich—a kind of loose-meat burger—is for all the world more like papier mâché than beef. But the place was where we ate, and the food was what we ate when we were there. We talked and laughed, as much as anything about the food, and that was why we liked it.

And we liked it because of how the place was run: the service was as bad as the food. During one particularly memorable week, Vic and I pulled into the Tastee Inn and ordered our lunches at the little microphone set up at the end of the drive. I ordered a Tastee sandwich, chocolate malt, and fries; Vic ordered a fish sandwich, large diet Coke, and onion chips, double dip. When we pulled up to the pick-up window, I got my bag—Tastee, malt, fries—and Vic got his—a cup of chili, two chili dogs, and a lemonade. As we paid, Vic mentioned that this wasn't exactly, or even close to, what he'd ordered, but, oh well, it would do.

The next day we were back again, and I ordered two chili dogs, potato salad, and a medium Dr Pepper; Vic ordered two Tastees, onion chips, and a cup of coffee. When we pulled up to the window, I got my bag—dogs, salad, Pepper, and Vic got his—a fish sandwich, three french fries, and a lemonade. This time he complained a bit more forcefully. He said he'd eat the stuff he got, but, once again, it wasn't even close to what he had ordered.

Third day, same thing. I got exactly what I wanted; Vic got not a single thing he had asked for. He snapped. He pushed the bag back through the window and said that this time he would like to have what he wanted to have when he had placed his order only moments before. I imagine he expected an apology. Maybe he forgot we were at the Tastee. The elderly lady inside the window snatched the sack from his hands, leaned out the window and into his face, and snarled, "What's the matter with you anyway, Mister? *You never get your order right.*" And from that moment on the Tastee Inn occupied a special place in our hearts.

SOUP DU JOUR

I love soup. I make a lot of soup. There are reasons for that, too. I am a notorious salvager. I throw nothing away. We compost everything from our kitchen. We save all aluminum. I use discarded containers in my shop. No scrap of cloth is thrown out without finding another use first around the farm. We live in an abandoned house that we salvaged and rebuilt. My hobby is restoring old tractors delivered to and abandoned in junkyards for scrap iron. My career was as a folklorist, collecting old ideas—stories, barns, songs, knowledge, philosophies—tossed out by the mainstream culture. So when I boil up my ribs, or when Linda boils a ham, I'm sure as hell not going to throw that rich broth down the drain! I save it to make soup.

I suppose part of my enchantment with soup comes from my early associations with the Omaha Indians. Somewhere down the line I'm going to tell you about Native American foodways, but for the moment it's important only that you know that every Indian gathering involves the sharing of food—called a feast, even though sometimes the fare is pretty modest for a *feast*. So, there's going to be some sort of gathering, and there is going to be some food. Whoever is throwing the affair gets together a couple dozen chickens, or a pig, or a few pounds of inexpensive cuts of beef—maybe some stew meat or a couple roasts. Or an old milk cow gotten from the market as a cutter-and-canner. Now, you have no idea how many people are going to show up for this event. Could be anywhere from twenty to a hundred. And as is always the case at Native American gatherings, everyone from hulks like me to little kids get the same amount of food—sometimes not much more than a snack, sometimes so much you take a few pounds of yummies home with you.

So what can you make with that meat that will take care of any number of people and allow equal division no matter how many guests show up? SOUP! All the meat is cut up, usually in half-fist-size hunks, no matter what the cut.

Visitors to Indian gatherings come away with the idea that Indians must cut up their beef for serving with dynamite or a chain saw, because there sure isn't much subtlety about it. Then the meat is boiled in a big pot of water. Can't get simpler than that. If there's some rice or macaroni from the last commodity allotment, toss that in, too. That's Indian soup.

I've already admitted that food is a lot more than food, and I suppose this is one of those times when food is terrific because of all the good memories connected with it, which may strike someone without such memories as pretty dull stuff. But I like it, yes, I do. I add other stuff too—Linda's favorite secret ingredient (mashed potatoes), and carrots and celery, soup standards. But soup is forgiving stuff, and it'll all be gone in a couple days anyway, so it offers a perfect opportunity for culinary adventure. Jerry Seinfeld says the biggest advantage of soup is that it is already half digested. In fact, he says, he is looking forward to Campbell's coming out with a line of IV soups. Well, okay, maybe that's one of the reasons I love the stuff so much—it doesn't take much work to eat it.

A few weeks ago, I was hungry for soup, so I dug around in the freezer and found a couple packages of beef neck bones—perfect for soup, not good for much of anything else. I boiled them up, pretty much all day. The next morning, when it had cooled, I skimmed the fat from the top of the pot and picked what little meat there was off the bones. I added sliced carrots and celery, some garlic and sliced onion, and, um, let's see, what else is in the fridge? Some leftover ham loaf. Okay, so that goes in. Mashed potatoes from supper last night. Super. In it goes. And hey, look at this! In the freezer is a bag of ten or twelve onion rings from our visit to Burger King yesterday. Throw 'em in, breading and all. And a couple slices of cheese, getting a little on the woody side. Dice it.

In it goes. Some fresh garlic from the cupboard. A dash of season salt to taste.

The result? Incredible. Some of the best soup I've ever had, no kidding. The downside is that I'll never have that soup again. But that's okay. I had it once, didn't I? Isn't that worth remembering? This American-McDonald's notion that all food has to be exactly the same, every time, every place, is nonsense. ("Well, uh, yeah, I'd order that soup du jour except the idiots never can get it the same two days in a row!") You know, European cookbooks don't have proportions in them. A German soup recipe would read a little like mine: Take some meat, celery, carrots, cheese, onion, garlic, and onion rings. Mix them together. Prepare as you would any soup. That's it. That's all you need.

I used to make wine. A lot of wine. I'd come up with a few gallons, maybe a few dozen gallons of some really good wine, and I got pretty good at it. I'd bottle it and keep it in the cellar, enjoying it with meals and friends with abandon. But the going got tough when I got toward the bottom of any particular good vintage. There's no way to duplicate the fruit that went into that wine or its condition or the temperature at which it was fermented or the yeast that turned the sugar into alcohol or anything else. And yet wine has a relatively short life. Only the very best wines handle long aging well, so there was no sense in trying to hold back bottles for years. The stuff I was making was good, but it sure wasn't a Baron Rothschild Première Cru! The supply would dwindle down to a half-dozen bottles, and then a couple. Eventually the last bottle would make its way to our table, and I would toast that lovely wine and its gift to us, drink the glass . . . and it was gone, never to be tasted by me or anyone else ever again.

Plumb romantic, right? And maybe even a little sad. But

it's not exactly a tragedy. So it goes with soup and wine, with love and life. Forget recipes in all those complex brews. Drink deep. Carpe diem. Make that soup.

MUSICAL FRUIT

Especially if you elect to take advantage of another of my very most favorite foodstuffs—beans! I know that I am entering a culinary minefield here. Beans are one of those things, like opera, that are said to carry with them their own punishment, but I don't think men see it quite that way. It's pretty hard to talk about beans without at least *thinking* about farting, right? Especially since this book is about food and *men*. Ladies, maybe they teach you this at Woman School, I don't know. I can't even get my loving and trusting twelve-year-old daughter to tell me a thing about Woman School and I asked her again this very morning. But the thing is, men don't see farting as a problem. Not even offensive. Sure, they'll make a big display of waving their hands and running out of the room into a cold night by way of dramatizing a really good human pickled-egg-and-beer fart, or maybe the offerings of a couple big dogs who earlier in the day did away with a bunch of squirrel stew, but that's ritual, not culture. I suspect you know that. Maybe it's historical: no scene in movie literature of the American West more clearly captures an absolute truth than the campfire meal scene from Mel Brooks's *Blazing Saddles*. That's probably why they've muted the entire passage for television—too close to the truth.

I don't know if women fart, either, but I suspect that they do. Buddy Hackett has apparently the same suspicions: Buddy once noted that he has observed women don't fart . . . but often stand near dogs that do. Little girls fart. Do they lose the ability with age? I'd be the last to know. My daughters in their youth actually rejoiced at my recitations of classical, philosophical poetry along this line:

Beans, beans, the musical fruit,
The more you eat, the more you toot;
The more you toot, the better you feel,
So let's eat beans for every meal!

When two of my daughters, Joyce and Jenny, were much younger, they got to giggling in the backseat of my mom's car and she tried to quiet them down, asking what was going on. Joyce explained that Jenny had farted. My mother then explained that ladies don't say *fart*. One of the girls of course inquired what ladies do say, and Mom explained, "Ladies say *fluff*." Maybe that's it: Women fluff.

I have encountered formulae for taking the anger out of beans. The most successful—and it is only modestly effective—has been to add a couple teaspoons of baking soda to the water during the first boiling of a batch of beans. It turns the water a terrible yellow, and you don't want to use much, because it affects the taste of the beans—and not to the better. I recommend that you make your beans and bean soup at a time when you are free to enjoy the full resonance and music of beans at their natural best. Cooked carrots, on the other hand, I can do without; they agitate a man's bodily furies to discomfort, I find. Dogs won't touch 'em. Speaking of which, has anyone ever done research on why dogs generate only SBDs? Is it a result of being bun-deficient? Are they harkening back to a time when unnecessary noises might draw larger predators in the wild? Wouldn't smells do the same thing? Or are the smells another defense mechanism? God knows, that's been my experience.

And God, it has become clear to me, does indeed know. A number of incredibly wise Indians—Oliver Saunsoci, Sr., Richard Fool Bull, Calvin Iron Shell, and Buddy Gilpin, among others—have pointed out to me that there are things we human beings can know,

if we want to hear and see. But the white man is educated out of hearing and seeing such things and therefore misses a lot. As one of my wise Native American mentors put it, "You white guys sure put a lot of faith in coincidence!"

For example, I once was working on a script, and I talked with a guy who has spent a good part of his life researching ancient strains of beans, the kinds raised by Indians of this area centuries ago—you know, the real colorful ones. Well, that was interesting. So I went uptown to the tavern and found a bunch of my old buddies sitting around talking . . . about the old Indian beans folks used to grow around here— you know, the real colorful ones. An hour later I came home to find my friend Jim Harrison had sent me a package from Arizona. You guessed it: ten pounds of assorted Indian beans. You know, the real colorful ones.

Coincidence, right? Oh, yeah, sure. So, what would you do in a situation like that? Shrug your shoulders and say, "Small world, ain't it?" Not me and my Indian buddies. I made some beans, right then and there. I don't know why. Something just told me that's what I should do.

Bean Soup

I have tried various methods of boiling beans to hasten the process of baking or cooking them as soup, including the baking powder notion. I don't recommend them. Stick with the old tried-and-true method of soaking them overnight, washing them carefully, draining them, soaking them again. How can you tell when they are softened? Eat one. Raw beans are delicious. When you start, you may have doubts about whether you have enough in that pot. Believe me, you do. Those beans are going to swell up to three or four times the volume you see right now.

I save the water I take off hams, hocks, ribs, whatever, and freeze it in empty milk cartons. When I'm ready to make soup, I take out a quart or two of my frozen stock, heat it up, add the soaked beans— anywhere between a half and a full cup, and add some meat—beef to beef stock, pork to pork stock, of course. I like to add some of my ham to pork stock, but I toss in a meaty bone, some bacon (buy a cheap package of bacon ends), whatever I've rounded up. For beef, I like neck bones or oxtail, although I like to boil those cuts separately and then add them to the soup later so I can more easily sort out the bones.

I like to throw in onions, celery, mashed potatoes, french fries, onion rings, garlic, garlic powder, whatever strikes my fancy along that line, whatever I have in the fridge or cupboard.

Cook the whole mess slowly for a good half day, but if you have more time, why not let the stuff perk away? Then I let the soup cool overnight. I don't usually plan on eating the soup the day I cook it for two reasons: (1) soup is always better when it's had a chance to sit for a day or two—ALWAYS! and (2) in the morning you can ladle off the coagulated fat. I'm not fussy about such things, but soup fat really doesn't add much to the mix. It's the stock *flavor* you're after from the meat, not the fat. You can put leftover soup back into the milk boxes and freeze it for later if you want, but I think soup just gets better the longer it stands around, so I let it stand around. After a while, after being warmed a couple times, the beans fall apart into a homogeneous mess and are just terrific.

Baked Beans

Prepare your beans pretty much the same as I describe in the first paragraph above. Then boil them a few hours in water (rather than stock). Drain them and add new water. Now add cut-up bacon, ham hocks, Spam, wienies, old pork chops, bacon ends, fatback, sowbelly, etc. Chop in some onions, but I like to wait until the very end to add some onion so they keep their crunchy texture. That may be too much trouble for you. Mix in a bottle or two of barbecue sauce. Some people like catsup, but I think it's too bland. I even add some Tabasco sauce or salsa to liven up the barbecue sauce. Add brown sugar or molasses to taste. Consider goodies like peppers. Know what's really good in baked beans? Apple slices.

If the mixture seems a little dry for prolonged baking, add a bottle of beer. Consider soy sauce, Worcestershire sauce, steak sauce, tomato juice, V8, Bloody Mary mix, whatever, as you like.

Nestle this mixture nicely in the pot you are going to bake it in—my favorite device is a big, cast-iron Dutch oven, which I then prefer to cook in the fireplace on a cold winter day. I like the economy of cooking soup in the winter, too, so the heat used in cooking (not to mention the perfume of the beans) adorns the house. Layer the top with more bacon strips, bacon ends, ham slices, pork chops, or—this is fun!—apple or pineapple slices. I've also tried cheese, but that can be a little messy when you're serving. Look around; see what you have.

Bake the beans for a few hours, at about 350°. The beans may get a little crusty around the edges and on the top, especially if you use the uneven heat of a campfire or fireplace, but the crusty parts are the best. Hint: if you use the fireplace, turn the pot occasionally to even out the heat, and don't try fireplace cookery with anything but cast iron. The cast iron helps distribute the heat evenly.

As I mentioned above, I like to add diced or sliced onion shortly before serving so the onions are hot and cooked but still crunchy.

Caution:

Beans are terrific but they may not be a great romance food, if you catch my drift, unless you are testing your date for marriage. Beans on a first date are a bad idea, but somewhere down the line they provide a significant testing ground for a longer or more intense relationship.

I'm having some organizational problems with this book at this point because I am gradually easing into another category, one that overlaps rather drastically with another, maybe forming a totally second layer of food purposes. Yes, a man should know how to make baked beans and bean soup for the survival of his body and therefore his species. And yes, there is solid evidence that a man needs the melody of beans to clear his mind and metabolism. And I was about to ease on over into spuds, another of the most wonderful of foods for a man, but . . .

The problem is, I am *talking* about basic survival foods but I am *thinking* about performance. You can make bean soup or baked beans or any of the potato dishes I'm going to talk about down the line, but the thing is, you can also come to think of one particular kind of beans or potatoes, or soup for that matter, as *yours,* a specialty you have become famous for, a dish others identify you with, something you carry to taverns and parties and homes where you want to make a special mark, a culinary specialty, a purpose, a *gift.*

BLUE-LIGHT SPECIALS

Dave Ratliff's chili is famous around here. No one else is comfortable making chili because it is generally understood that the only chili in the world is Dave's. Same with Harriett Nielsen's potato soup. Oh, you can make potato soup at home and eat it and enjoy it just fine, but you sure as hell wouldn't waltz into the town tavern with a pot of potato soup and not expect everyone to notice it's good, but "it isn't Harriett's potato soup." Sue Halsey makes green chili, but that's different. Dave makes Texas chili. I once thought it would be fun and personally beneficial to organize a potato soup contest at the local tavern, me serving as judge and eating all the potato soup I want, and I want potato soup a lot. What I failed to realize is that you can joke about a woman's husband, with some caution even her children, but you better watch your step when it comes to her cooking! Three years later I'm still getting snarly remarks around town about awarding the steward of the town dump first prize in that blasted soup contest.

Anyway, somewhere along here you need to start thinking about your specialty. Every man needs one—something you feel confident about cooking, something you can do in other people's kitchens, something distinctive, something you like. And you don't want to make it very often. Dad and I once made the mistake of telling Mom we liked this cinnamony, coconutty cake she made. So she made another one the next day, and like idiots we praised it again, and ate it. About the fifth cake that month we were still trying to be diplomatic, and so six or eight weeks into this cake marathon we finally had to break the word that we'd had just about all that cake we could handle, maybe the rest of our lives. It's the only time I can remember seeing my mother cry. Dad and I learned something from that, and I suspect Mom did, too. When you make something good, and everyone praises you about it, make 'em beg for it the next time.

In fact, if you're cooking for one particular group over a long period of time, it's worth remembering that nothing lasts longer than poor cooking. A bad stew will hang around for weeks. My pal Barre Toelken tells the story about a crew of loggers who had an arrangement that whoever complained about the food instantly became the camp cook. So, no matter what the fare, you wanted to be careful not to grouse, because you'd wind up over the hot stove, putting together the next meal for the boys.

Well, this one guy was the camp cook for months. It's not that he was such a good cook; thing is, no one else wanted the job. In desperation, one day he baked up a moose turd pie, figuring that that should gain his relief from kitchen subservience forever. He served up that moose turd pie, and the boys dug in. As you can imagine, the reaction was instantaneous. One fellow, unable to restrain himself, blurted out, "Sweet Jesus, this tastes like moose turds . . . ," but then, realizing the potential consequences of his error, took another bite and added, "Good, though."

As far as I can tell, potatoes are just about the perfect survival food because they are not only easy to cook, but easy to cook *well*. I think it would take an encyclopedia to put together all the ways spuds can be prepared for the table, and they're all good, as far

as I'm concerned. I've spoken of the sexual allure of mashed potatoes, and Pop's Rooshen fries, but for most men, it's the baked potato that is probably paramount. Wrap a potato in aluminum foil or mud or leaves or wet paper or whatever, and throw it in the fire or on the grill or in the oven or onto the manifold, and you got food. You want fancy food? Add sour cream, gravy, butter, cheese, for all I know, peanut butter. It tastes good. Breakfast, lunch, supper, doesn't matter. Picnic, banquet, who cares? There's not a doubt in my mind that if Jesus did indeed come to North America before Columbus as the Mormons preach, at his last supper here, he offered up Kentucky bourbon and Idaho potatoes.

One of the reasons this book is to be read only by men is that I'm not sure it would be a good idea for the next male secret to fall into the hands of someone on the faculty of Woman School. The one thing men crave more than anything else from a woman is . . . surprise! . . . mashed potatoes. I have interviewed maybe five hundred single men and as many married men whose wives don't understand them, and while some mentioned something else lacking in their lives but flourishing in their fantasies, mashed potatoes was *always* right up there. Any woman can, well, you know, but only a few can make mashed potatoes. My Lovely Linda's mashed potatoes are second to none. It may throw the balance of power between men and women out of whack for men to have this recipe and therefore not have a hell of a lot of need for women anymore, thus bringing about the destruction of the human race as we know it, but here it is anyway.

Linda's Man-Magnet Mashed Potatoes

So, if the Numero Uno reason a man marries a woman is for her mashed potatoes, why I am bothering to include the ultimate mashed potato recipe here, where women can easily find and ruthlessly wield it? Reason #1: Because this book is for men only. Reason #2: Because now that *you* have the recipe, you can make your own mashed potatoes. And move on to Numero Two-o reason why a man marries a woman more quickly, that's why.

6 medium potatoes (treat yourself to new potatoes whenever possible). Peel, quarter, and cover with cold water in a four-quart pot.

When ready to cook, drain water and again add enough COLD (trust me on this) water to just cover the potatoes.

Add dash of salt, cover pot, and bring to a boil.

Reduce heat and boil, covered, for 20 minutes.

Drain, reserving one cup or so of potato water to use in making gravy from pan drippings if you're having meat as an entrée.

Whip the potatoes with margarine (2 tablespoons or according to taste), about 1/2 cup milk (more or less), and, optionally, about 2 teaspoons minced onion or 1/2 teaspoon minced garlic. [Author's note: These ingredients are not optional, no matter what Linda says. In fact, go for both.]

Whip until smooth. Serves 3–4 [Author's note: Or maybe two]. Any leftover mashed potatoes can be put into the starting liquid for homemade soup. [Author's note: AND HOW!]

I love popcorn, and when I need a quick meal, that's what I make. I had a friend who once made popcorn his specialty dish. I use a lot of his techniques, but what's important here is that he didn't need anything special that someone wouldn't have in most cupboards. So, if there was an appropriate time for a snack, he would pipe up, "If you have some popcorn, I could make some. I take special pride in my way around a popcorn popper. All I need is a large pot, some margarine or butter, a slice of bacon, season salt, and a piece of aluminum foil." And he was on his way. He made a lot of friends that way. His trick is aluminum foil. His popcorn theory is that a tight pan keeps the moisture in and makes for tough popcorn. So you want to let the steam escape as it exits the corn, as easily as possible. He covered the pan with aluminum foil and poked it full of holes with a large meat fork or paring knife.

Popcorn

I thoroughly like my Flecknor Movie Theater Popcorn popper. It's a roughly two-quart stainless-steel pot with a complex lid on it. The lid has a geared handle, so you turn a crank, and it turns an axle that goes down into the center of the pot. At the end of the axle there is a paddle that scrapes the bottom of the pot, just like popcorn poppers in movie houses. It beats shaking a pan, and it really cuts down on old maids left in the bottom of the pan.

But let's say you're sticking to Ol' Rog's Simplicity Plan and you don't have a Flecknor's popper. Any light, deep pan will do, and I do use my friend's perforated aluminum foil trick. I also like commercial popcorn oils, especially Orville Redenbacher's, although it is a little pricey. Any cooking oil will do. A spoon of bacon grease can really zest up the corn. (My Indian friends put bacon grease on roasting ears, also an interesting variation on an old standard.)

Make sure you have fresh popcorn. The stuff won't last forever. And it's not that expensive, so if you find your popcorn getting smaller and smaller and tougher and tougher and there are more and more old maids in the bottom of the pan, dump the old stuff and buy a new package. The notion of "gourmet popcorn" seemed goofy to me for a long time but, you know, there really is a difference. We stick pretty much with plain old popcorn around here; gourmet stuff is better, but I don't think it's worth the price.

Pop the corn quickly at high heat and get it off the heat the moment the popping stops. I consider my popcorn a gesture toward weight control, so I don't load it up with butter, as much as I love it that way. I use artificial butter flavoring (not butter-flavored *salt*, which tends to load up your popcorn too much with salt). I like Pop'n Topper a lot. Then comes the real secret: I "salt" my popcorn with a dash of Lowry's Season Salt. I think it makes the corn taste better, but I also think its strong flavor lets me use less salt. Or how about cayenne red pepper? Wow!

I have also flavored my popcorn with grated cheese—for example, grated Parmesan cheese topping packaged for pasta dishes. If you get it on the popcorn while the corn is still hot so it sticks, it's terrific.

Yes, there's a problem that someone might steal your techniques, but most of the time, if you are generous with your offerings, folks will leave your specialties up to you. Another friend of mine considered shish kebabs to be his forte. When he was going to cook, he brought a little box of his own fixin's, and he demanded that he be left alone in the kitchen while he worked his ways. The shishes weren't all that great, but again, most of the time people will humor you if you are doing the cooking and if you make it clear that this is not just a matter of food but a major culinary performance. And if they complain, they have to cook next time.

Kebabs

Kebabs are nice, because they actually don't require much in the way of special equipment or materials. Sure you need meat, but just about anything from filets to wienies will do; spuds (you might want to bake or boil them before skewering them for the grill, since they are not likely to cook as quickly as everything else); peppers, onions, squash, and whatever else you can get to stick on the skewer. I marinade my meat for shish kebabs pretty much the same as for ribs. These are also good for fireplace cookery.

I definitely prefer beef for kebabs but I have also used boneless cuts of chicken. I'm not all that confident about my kebabs. They're good, but I don't think I have any secrets, and I certainly haven't mastered them. I do like to use iron skewers rather than wood because I think they carry heat to the center of the meat, but any stick will do, especially over a campfire. Eat the stuff with your fingers or directly from the skewer, and you have fewer dishes to wash. Maple, mulberry, or cottonwood is better than turpentiney pine, however—

as you can imagine—and poison ivy is never a good culinary choice.

To be sure the meat is well cooked on the grill, I boil it briefly beforehand. As is the case with my ribs, the meat is pretty well cooked by the time I put it on the skewers. (Don't forget to save the broth for soup!) The grilling is mostly to warm it and add the flavor of smoke. (Also as mentioned above, I bake or boil my spuds—usually new potatoes—in advance of skewering.) I like to marinate the meat twenty-four hours in advance of cooking, using the marinade I outlined above for ribs.

If I have any special technique at all, it's that I do insist on alternating nonmeat and meat pieces—onion wedge, meat, pepper, meat, pineapple, meat, spud, meat, that sort of thing. If I'm not that long on meat, that's okay; I just alternate the nonmeats—onion, spud, pineapple, onion, meat, spud, onion, pepper. . . . It blends flavors.

After the skewered goodies are hot, I slather them again with sauce. I have the impression the sauce sticks better to hot stuff. When we serve kebabs, we empty the skewers into a common bowl from which everyone serves themselves.

Up to this point we've looked at nice little favorites you can toss together almost any time, anywhere, on the spur of the moment. Another buddy of mine has made whole hogs his special talent. Whenever he's invited to a party, if it seems at all appropriate, he asks, "Need a hog?" And if the answer is positive, he shows up a day early with everything from shovels to gunnysacks, bushels of vegetables to a dead hog, a quarter cord of firewood to huge knives and forks for cutting up the finished product. I don't know his recipe, if he has one, so I can't include it, even in a sidebar. I suppose it would start with "Take one hog. . . ."

It's been years since I've watched him in action, but essentially all we did was dig a pit big enough to hold the hog. We built a fierce hardwood fire in the pit (mulberry wood is what we used, and it burned like coal), and let it blaze for hours until it was down to a deep bed of coals. We shoveled a mess of the coals into an old washtub while we put the hog in the pit. This guy usually scrubbed the butchered but whole hog with a wire brush, but did not skin it, and stuffed it full of peppers, potatoes, onions, a cabbage or two, carrots, turnips—just about anything handy. He preferred to wrap the hog in wet burlap bags, but this was something of short notice—he had a hog die on the way to market, and he knew we were working outside building a cabin, so he just hauled the hog over, and we cooked it on the spot with no notice—so, as I recall, he wrapped it in sodden clay mud and wet newspapers, tied on with an entire roll of cotton grocery string we had been using for plumb line, chalk line, that kind of thing. We dropped the hog into the fire pit and poured the remainder of the hot coals over the hog. It was a ferocious fire, so there were plenty of coals. He put a couple hunks of mulberry wood under the hog and over it, right in with the coals, and then we covered the whole thing with soil—in this case, mostly sand.

This was all in the dark of night, us stumbling around trying to get the fire just right and all, and we didn't get the whole thing tucked away until the early hours of the morning. The next day, every so often my friend went over to the pit, now a steaming mound, and dumped a bucket or two of water right over the top of it. The water soaked through the sand easily, and, almost instantly, there would be an explosion of steam and little geysers of hot water bubbling up through the surface. He explained that the meat was not so much baking as it was steaming. Later the next day, almost thirty-six hours after he'd shown up with the dead hog in the first place, we dug up the pit. The mud, paper, and hog were still very, very hot, and as hard as a brick. Getting that brute out of the pit was a real job.

There were maybe a dozen people helping me on the cabin project and there was general dismay when we finally got the hog out of the pit. We'd been working hard, anticipating that pork, egged on by my friend's bragging about how great he was at this hog-cooking thing. All we could see was a huge, muddy, steaming, charred mess. The baked and blackened clay and newspaper fell off to reveal a thoroughly burned pig, black as tar, hard as the brick-and-paper envelope around it. And that was all we had planned to eat for the day, so the disappointment was genuine.

"Now, don't give up on me here," our friend insisted, digging out his gigantic tools—forks as big as pitchforks, spoons like shovels. He began hacking, sawing, and heaving at that carcass, and whoa! Just under that charred skin was . . . beautiful, fragrant, moist roast pork, steaming and pretty. He handed each member of his cynical audience a hunk of pork on the end of his long fork, and the skepticism stopped. While we juggled the meat from hand to hand to keep from getting permanent burn scars, we ate, and oh, how we ate. We ate pork, squash, potatoes, onions—I think there were even a couple roasted pineapples and bananas for dessert in the collection. Thing is, it was not just food; it was a magic act. Just when we were at the brink of despair, maybe even

anger, we were jerked back by the masterful per-
former, who was now everyone's hero. That's what
having a food specialty can do for you.

Of course there are perils in such pride. Boom
John Carter once came to a New Year's Eve celebration at the same cabin, full of elaborate boasting about how
he was going to treat us to his specialty New Year's Day
morning—huevos rancheros. Some of us were excited about
the notion of a morning feast. Others remembered the time
Boom John was going to fix Cornish hens on his new grill. At
one in the morning we were still sitting around waiting for
the damned things to get done, and then something went
wrong and the whole mess caught fire, eventually burning
the hinges off the grill. (I took home the charred rubble, since
I was divorce-poor at the time and needed a grill in any condition for myself, which is where I got started with the
square, flattish grills I have come to prefer, except with
hinges. Even without hinges it was the best grill I'd ever
used.)

So doubt about John's promised breakfast was running
high.

Doubt, however, was the least of our emotions when
Boom John went noisily to work on his huevos on New
Year's morning, just a little before sunrise. My cabin is one
smallish room, and there were maybe fifteen of us, so we
were all, as it were, right in the middle of his cooking preparations. The banging of pots and pans roughly five hours
after you went to sleep and easily five hours before you
intend to get up again, all on a morning when the temperature is subzero outdoors, not much better indoors, and everyone has a champagne hangover, is not what most people
want on New Year's morning, if any morning. Our disposi-
tions were not helped by the fact that the evening before,

Boom John had anything but lived up to his name, falling asleep leaning back against the wall in his chair, at maybe, oh, 10 P.M.

Well, he *was* cooking, after all, and there *is* that moose turd pie story. . . . Boom John has a fondness for hot sauce, so he slathered his eggs, peppers, and meat generously with it. We drank a lot of his coffee, therefore, even though it had been boiled a bit much (coffee should never be boiled at all, in case you don't know), and so it was a little oily. Is any of this starting to fall together for you? All of those ingredients started working on us and our stomachs. And there were twelve or fifteen of us, all in a cabin. With an outdoor toilet maybe fifty paces away through the snow and subzero cold.

Pretty soon the parade to the outhouse started. Then people started putting on their warm clothes so they would be ready on deck when the last dyspeptic adventurer returned from his arctic trials. Then desperate people started piling up outside the cabin door, waiting for the first glimpse of the prior departure leaving the outhouse. And cold, wet people and clothing started piling up in the cabin, trying to warm up and dry off. Through all of this, of course, Boom John remained cheerfully undisturbed in spirit and body, blissfully unaware of the distress he had caused and the growing plot to burn him and his huevos rancheros recipe on a pyre somewhere between the cabin and the outhouse, where we could enjoy the warmth and his cries for mercy as we continued our regular rounds in and out.

I don't know if Boom John still considers huevos rancheros his specialty, but I know a bunch of folks who can be brought to tears of regret just remembering them. I can tell you one thing for sure, after those damned things, the rest of the year had to get better.

Boom John Carter's Huevos Rancheros, Act One

Let this be a lesson to you: there is an inherent danger in asking someone for his special recipe; this thing is a meal ticket, a matter of pride, access to women, acceptance among his peers. In fact, it is dangerous to ask a man for any kind of recipe. Men don't cook by recipes, and, in fact, don't even quite understand what a recipe is supposed to do. Take Boom John. I wrote to him and asked him if I could have the recipe for his famous huevos rancheros (flattery, I calculated, couldn't hurt). And he called me back and left a message on my answering machine that if I called him back he would tell it to me.

Now think about that. He was going to call me and tell me his recipe. Here's a guy, Boom John, who couldn't simply and accurately convey the size of his socks to me over the telephone, and he's going to give me a finely tuned formula that has maybe ten or twelve ingredients measured in tablespoons, teaspoons, cups, ounces, and pinches—a recipe for something someone might actually eat. And the only time he would be able to do this is about 7 P.M., when he's about halfway through a twelve-pack and I'm finishing off a bottle of young (but not presumptuous) merlot.

"Whaz that? Didju say 'one teaplespoon of Tabasco' or 'one season of tobacco'? I guess iduznd madder. An' whaz that a 'full jar of balsa' or a 'tool car of guavas'? An' you're sure this feeds fifteen, ride? Oh, fifty? How can fifteen eggs feed thirty? Oh, *fifty* eggs . . . "

You get the idea.

So, Boom John probably won't send me his recipe: (1) he doesn't want to share it; and (2) he doesn't know how to share it, because (3) he doesn't see his huevos rancheros as something reducible to writing on paper. My impression of the dish, however, is that you break a mess of eggs—the number doesn't particularly matter. Then you slice and dice a mess of onions, peppers, and mushrooms—again no particular number or type—and mix them in with the eggs. A little milk would be nice. How about last night's refried beans? Some hamburger, sausage, baloney, Spam, wienies, lutefisk (just kidding)? Sure, what the hell?! Add a jar or two of hot salsa, and then for good measure, some Tabasco sauce. If it were up to me, I'd want to add these things later, when the eggs are cooked, so I could get some idea just how badly my guests are going to be injured when they eat this stuff, but my impression is that Boom John doesn't think that way. He adds salsa and Tabasco until it *feels* right—not in his fingers as he stirs, or even to what it looks like, but how it resonates with his culinary karma. It was Chili Dave who came up with the watchword, "Anything worth doing is worth overdoing," but when it comes to salsa and Tabasco in breakfast eggs, Boom John *could* have said it.

You put all this stuff in a big, heavy black cast-iron pan over a hot fire and stir to beat hell. Pretty soon the mix starts to lump up, and then things happen fast. Keep scraping and stirring and start yelling for people to grab their plates and belly up to the stove. Don't let it bother you that it's 6 A.M. on New Year's morning and they're still in bed. Don't be deterred by the shouts of "John, you idiot, would you cut out the noise and throw that crap you're cooking outside, where the EPA can deal with it?" and "What did we do with that damned shotgun last night? Do we have any more shells?"

Put the pan on the table, where everyone can help themselves once they get in the spirit of the New Year. In the meanwhile, maybe you should make a quick trip to the outhouse before . . . well, it just might be a good idea to go now.

Boom John Carter's Huevos Rancheros, Act Two

I no sooner steeled my resolve not to receive Boom John's recipe when he rose to the embarrassment of not being included here and sent the following, which, like a hand grenade, is self-explanatory.

"First you find yourself some fresh, lean pork. I am told that traditionally it is best if the pig was stolen. Three to four pounds will feed the masses. Carefully trim as much fat from the meat as your patience will allow. The less, the better. [Author's note: I don't know whether he means the less trimming or the less fat, but knowing John, he probably doesn't, either.] Then chop the meat into tasty morsels. Actually, the proportion should be a morsel and a half to allow for shrinkage during cooking.

"Next, the secret ingredient. Go to your grocery store and buy a large jar of Pace's picante sauce. Back home, drag out the trusty Crock-Pot and at about ten o'clock in the evening combine the meat and the sauce and set the heat on medium. Retire.

"The next morning, prepare to awaken to an aroma that will coax a slug-a-bed from the sheets. [Author's note: Not to mention a slug-a-poop out of the house.]

Remove the lid from the pot for about an hour to allow the stock to reduce. If you were lazy in the trimming process, ladle off the excess grease.

"Purists then prepare a large tortilla, either by warming it on a heated skillet or by popping it in the microwave for about twenty seconds. Of late, revisionists have been substituting corn bread, which does have something to recommend it.

"While the tortilla is warming, prepare two eggs to taste. I think they are best when fried sunny-side up, so the yolks are quite runny. Take the tortilla and fold it in half. Then place the eggs on one half and drench them with the pork and sauce. A large dollop of life-giving, cholesterol-rich sour cream graces the heap, and then fold. Another ladling of pork and sauce over the top completes the assemblage.

"The meal experience is enhanced by appropriate side dishes. We recommend assorted fruits: apples, bananas, oranges. Avoid grapefruit for obvious reasons. [Author's note: Are the reasons obvious to you? Not to me.] These additions are collectively known as 'antidote.' Recommended beverages are coffee and juice. Milk is contraindicated as lactic acid curdles when brought into contact with the combination of sauce and gastric juices. Water is best left to finger bowls.

"There are some options to be considered. The picante sauce comes in three intensities. I think medium works best. The hot is tasty but causes long lines at the bathroom. It does make a nice substitute for commercial fumigation, however. The mild sauce is like sex with a condom. [Author's note: ?]

"For the health-conscious, substitute Egg Beaters for

the real thing—they are amazingly good—and phony sour cream—which is somewhat disappointing. We calculated this to be both a low-calorie breakfast and, as they say, 'heart smart.' There is a vegetarian version where you substitute Cheerios for the pork, but it isn't the same. In my old age I have gotten clever enough to buy the pork in largish lots, which is easier to trim. I then freeze three or four batches' worth. On a cold night you just pop the frozen pork in the Crock-Pot and off you go."

[Author's note: And that certainly is my recollection of the experience: "Off you go."]

Personal food specialties come in many forms and flavors. Sue Halsey makes brandies and wines. Another friend, now living in England, used to make a Christmas chutney. Old Ray Harpham used to come around our place every summer with another batch of tall tales and a jar of his famous—infamous?—horseradish sauce, and now that he's gone, we miss him all the more because we can no longer enjoy that liquid fire of his. At Christmas Shirley Carter makes . . . I don't know what to call it . . . a relish, I think, of peppers, carrots, pickles, and okra, in a spiced herbal oil—olive oil, I think. I nurse the stuff all year long, adding more carrots as I take hers out.

Mom Carter's Hotsy-Totsy Relish

I wondered about this: Why is it that I'm including a woman's recipe, even if it is Mom Shirley Carter's, in a book about men and food? This relish is terrific, however, so I did it—I asked her for the recipe. And the truth came out. It isn't Mom Carter's. It's Bill Grahn's, and he doesn't call it a relish. He's a man. He calls it Sexy Carrots. And here it is. I'll bet when it was just Bill Grahn's Sexy Carrots and not Mom Carter's Hotsy-Totsy Relish, there wasn't any of this 1/3 cup and one 4-oz. jar stuff, either.

1 cup cider vinegar
1 cup sugar
1/3 cup oil
2 lbs. small or sliced carrots
1 lb. sliced mushrooms
1 4-oz. jar diced pimiento, drained
1 cup chopped green onions
1 green or red pepper, diced
1 jar sliced jalapeño peppers, juice and all

I have also added a drained can of sliced water chestnuts.

Boil vinegar, sugar, and oil until sugar dissolves. Cool. Add vegetables. Refrigerate. Stir occasionally. Will keep a week or more. You may add more vegetables as you go along.

I also have my questions about the phrase "will keep a week or more." I keep Shirley's Christmas jars of this carrot relish all year long, eating, adding, adding, eating. I'm still eating some of her relish that's damn near two years old. Every time I take some, Linda says, "Roger, that stuff is so old, it's going to kill you." That's what a woman says. "Gets better every time I open the jar," I say. That's what a man says. Whatever the case, ignore that sentence in the recipe. This stuff is indestructible, and if you die from food poisoning, well, everyone's got to go sooner or later, and this beats a ruptured spleen.

EASY WAY OUT

A sneaky device that seems a food specialty but which may actually be a survival technique in disguise is the Favorite Condiment Ploy. Say you are going to visit a Danish or Norwegian family and you know that the food is going to be bland as tapioca and Aunt Betty's bread. Bring along not a bottle of wine or a hunk of Stilton, but a bottle of your favorite Tabasco sauce or mustard. You look like you're being generous with a gift, but actually you're thinking of your own palate at suppertime.

By the way, one of the most remarkable, memorable, and useful foods institutions in America is the Mount Horeb (Wisconsin) Mustard Museum. This place offers, by mail, hundreds of incredibly good mustards, dry and prepared, for every taste and budget. I've established a regular correspondence with these folks. When I give away my Christmas hams, I sometimes toss in a bag of exotic Russian mustard, in a paper bag with Cyrillic print all over it, or maybe a crockery pot of French mustard, so good you can eat it on toast. Contact the Mount Horeb Museum, get a catalog, order some mustard, and take some along the next time you're invited to supper at an uninteresting table. You'll never be made out to be such a hero when you're only taking care of yourself, you selfish little rascal.

I am currently enthusiastic about raising my own food. No, not gardening, for which I have never had sufficient patience, nor for gathering wild foods, which isn't always predictable, both in terms of yield or the reception you will get when you show up at your dinner host's door with an armload of young, succulent skunk cabbage. A couple of enterprising husbandrymen have come up with something I consider a contribution to mankind right up there with the bread machine: packaged mushroom gardens. In a space no bigger than the empty spot behind your toilet tank or under the basement stairs, you can grow luscious gourmet mushrooms. Just yesterday I took a can of very pedestrian soup (having not made any of my own for a spell) and as I warmed it on the stove, dropped in a large, gorgeous Portabello mushroom I grew in a box in my wine room a couple months ago and then kept in a plastic bag in the refrigerator freezer. Talk about a transformation! Then for supper I grilled burgers and tossed another Portabello cap on several of the patties. Yikes!

You can grow Portabellos, regular, plain ol' button mushrooms, pom pom blancs, Sonoma browns, golden oysters, even shiitakes with an absolute minimum of effort on your part. You mix up some stuff to begin with, wet it down good, cut some plastic sheeting off, sprinkle or mist it every so often with water—each mushroom comes with directions and requires slightly different care—and pick the goodies when they are ready to go. The kits don't smell at all, are easily handled and clean, and the mushrooms, well, are superb.

Now, these delights are great enough for your own pleasure, but imagine the impression you're going to make when you show up at that flight attendants' party with a bag of fresh, delicious, earthy, musky, basic, fleshy (if you catch my drift) mushrooms! You're bound to get a rise. Or at your boss's dinner party. She'll think you're a genius. You're bound to get a raise. (So far I've tried the products of Redigro Mushrooms, PO Box 124, Hamburg, IA 19526 and Gourmet Mushrooms, PO Box 515, Graton, CA 95444 and they are both terrific. Gourmet even sells hunks of spawn and directions for planting it in your backyard so you can harvest the incredible morel mushroom right outside your back door. God, I love science!)

One more thing before I forget. My buddy Eric, up at the

tavern, is absolutely right when he says that when you find something you really like, whether it's a kind of mattress or a kind of mustard, buy all of it you can afford and have room for, because sure as hell, as soon as they figure out that it's good, they're going to quit making it. Yes, it's true, once a great product is developed and accepted by the public, they should make more of it. But they don't. They quit making it. Don't ask me why. Remember Jay Anderson? He and I were once in a rural tavern, reminiscing, and we got to talking about Greek food and Greek drink. We got to talking about ouzo, a heavy, sweet, anise liqueur, and man, the more we talked, the more we lusted after some ouzo. Well, we were in a town of 300 people, and one glance at the back bar convinced us we sure weren't going to find anything as exotic as ouzo here. In fact, there wasn't a town for 150 miles where we'd find ouzo, and maybe not there. But Jay said, "Wait a minute," and disappeared behind the bar. He talked with the bartender. They went into the kitchen, and emerged moments later with two glasses of clear liquid that smelled for all the world like ouzo.

There was one difference. This was *great* ouzo, the best I'd ever tasted or, for that matter, have tasted to this very day. I finally pried the secret out of Jay and barkeep, and it was simple enough; they had gone to the basement where there were a few bottles of the cheapest possible licorice schnapps, a specialty, it turned out, pretty much reserved for the cold hunting season when hunters carried a jug of the stuff with them into the field. Sort of to give the ducks and pheasants an extra advantage, I guess.

So I started buying Phillips Licorice Schnapps. The stuff cost five or six bucks a quart. Stinking cheap, luxuriously delicious. I bought it by the case, it was so good. Then one day I said to Eric, "Hey, buddy, pick me up another case of that licorice schnapps, okay?" and he said, "They don't make it anymore."

"You mean they don't have it in stock right now?"

"Don't make it."

"Maybe they won't have it then until hunting season?"

"Nope. Don't make it anymore. And they won't make anymore. It's like everything else that's good. They quit. I sold a billion gallons of that stuff out of here. Never could get enough. So they quit making it. That's it, Rog. Your licorice schnapps period just ended."

That's not a circumstance, either; it's a pattern. I love Jovan Musk soap. It smells good, feels good, washes well, and so I got to using it every day. But not for long. They quit making it, and now you can't get it. I love Sam's Choice flavored water, especially apple flavor. Perhaps it would be better to say I *did* love it, because they don't make it anymore. But then the cranberry filled in because it was pretty good, too. *Was*. Can't get it anymore. Same with plum. They have plenty of kiwi-strawberry, which I hate, however, and tropical fruit, which I loathe.

I understand somewhere in the world they do still make slivovitz, a fiery, Eastern European plum brandy. I'd drink it every day if I could get it. Nebraska distributors don't bring it into the state. Why? Because I like it, that's why. So buy stuff while you can, and don't stint on the proportions, whether it's mushroom kits or salsa.

Don't buy good mustard, good wine, good Tabasco, good anything by the bottle. Buy it by the metric ton, take it from me. Besides, there's something primal in excess. A woman about to have a baby begins to pad her nest. It's in her nature. Just watch. A man in charge of providing food for his family and clan does the same thing. Once, for example, a

Christmas present arrived from my buddy Boom John Carter. I opened it and found . . . a five-pound block of Stilton cheese, my favorite. Now, one eats little slivers of Stilton on bits of cracker and bread, right? It's rich and pungent and a system just can't handle too much of it at a time. At least that's what a woman would think. Not me. I tore John's gift from its box and bit hunks directly off the block as if I were tearing flesh from a freshly killed mammoth. Then, when the outcry from my family became too much for me, I wrenched off a slab and retreated to the wine cellar where I could wash it down with Port drunk directly from the bottle.

Linda suggested we should cut the block up into small pieces, put them in little plastic bags, and freeze them. That way we could enjoy moderate portions for many months to come. That would have been not only destruction of my glee at the obscenity of this cinder-block size bit of ecstasy but a clear violation of Boom John's intentions. If he had wanted me to have a bunch of little separate packages of cheese, that's what he would have sent. The point here was not Stilton, or five pounds of Stilton. This was all about ONE five-pound hunk of Stilton. It was not about savoring but devouring. The inevitable discomfort of excess was not seen by either the donor or donee as a repercussion or consequence, but as part and parcel of men and their ways with food. John knew I'd eat myself sick, and he anticipated that not for my discomfort but for my fulfillment; my dry heaves were never a chorus of curses for Boom John but a tribute to his generosity. (I had the remarkable opportunity the next morning of talking with both John and his lady, Annie; they both said I was precisely right about my conclusions. Except John was delighted to the point of giggling, and Annie was offended to the point of disgust.)

This is man-thinking. Men like beer in kegs. Or at least quart bottles. I buy half-gallon tins of Sapporo beer at the local tavern, in part so I can honestly tell Linda when I get home that I had only one beer, but also because I take pleasure in the volume of the huge container sitting on the bar before me.

I was once talking with Jim Taylor, in Houston. "Is there anything I can bring you when I come up?" he asked.

"Yeah," I said. "I sure could use some mesquite wood—some chips, maybe—for my barbecue."

"You got it," he said. But then he called and said he didn't have room for it in his car, but he'd send it. Then he said the post office wouldn't handle it. Then he said he had a friend coming this way with a truck and he'd bring it, dumping it in the yard if he happened to come by during the night. I was beginning to suspect something was up. Why wouldn't a packet of wood chips fit in Jim's car? Why wouldn't the post office handle it? Why was his friend bringing the wood in a *truck?* Was there some significance to the verb *dump?*

One morning not long after that exchange, I was leaving the house when I discovered that Jim's friend had indeed come through. During the night he had unloaded a gigantic iron basket of mesquite wood—maybe a quarter ton of the stuff—bound with steel straps to a pallet—in our driveway. And a fifty-pound bag of mesquite chips. And two cases of two-pound bags of chips. Jim had, in short, sent me a lifetime supply of mesquite.

And why not? Linda was dismayed, but I knew I could now rest easy for the rest of my life about this one very important thing. I might have health problems in my old age or encounter problems with wife and kin. I might run short of energy, tractor parts, cold beer, or patience, but for damn sure I'd never again have to worry about running short of mesquite for my smoker. Never, ever again, forever.

That's how men think. Jim's food specialty is gumbo. He makes gumbo and likes to share it with friends. He doesn't make a cup of gumbo, or a meal's worth. He doesn't share it with those who happen to be in his house. Or in his state. He's a man. Jim makes sixty gallons of gumbo at a time *and then FedExs it to his pals, of which I am delighted to be one.* Is it more trouble to make sixty gallons of gumbo than a quart? Is it more trouble to dish a cup of gumbo for a friend than ship four gallons five hundred miles? Is it more trouble to send a buddy 600 pounds of mesquite than two? Would I have been delighted with two ounces of Stilton? Of course! But it's not 240 or 250 times more trouble to send five pounds of Stilton. And the return on the investment is formidable. The impact, anecdotal value, and personal reputation enhancement of giving obscene quantities, especially of food-related stuff, is not simply more but is in fact incalculable. And to men, food is not a matter of nutrition but a matter of meaning; gratitude for God's gift of plenty, in a man's mind, is best recognized by a full measure of celebration of that plenty. Yea, unto a five-pound half wheel of Stilton!

ANYTHING WORTH DOING . . .

Men don't mind excess. They see it as putting away a little something for the future, a kind of culinary opportunism. And I think God wants it this way. I was once at a professional meeting in Texas and missed breakfast because I had an early morning breakfast. No big deal. I figured I'd catch a snack midmorning, or at worst get an early lunch before flying home. But the meeting lasted not only through the morning, but right up until the last moment I had to run to catch my plane. There were some snarls at the airport so I couldn't even grab a machine sandwich there, but what the heck, my ticket said there would be a meal served on the airplane, and this was back in the old days when they really did serve meals on airplanes. I was the last person onto the airplane and was seated in the last row.

My stomach was howling like a pack of starved badgers. Once in the air I watched the stewardesses (that's what they called them in the good ol' days) get the meals ready in the galley about five hundred yards away, in the front of the plane. And they started to serve. And precisely as I knew they would, they started serving at the front seats. An hour later they were back to me and I was in agony. Finally it was my turn. But what's this? She's coming back down the aisle . . . *with nothing in her hands.*

"Sir, I'm afraid I have some bad news."

"Ma'am, I sure hope it isn't that you're out of food, because I've been hungry now for about nine hours, and if I don't get food soon, I'm going to eat the back of this seat in front of me."

"Well, it's not quite that bad. We're out of salads, vegetables, and desserts"—long pause for dramatic effect—"but we have a couple dozen filets left, so I can give you all the steak you can eat. I'm dreadfully sorry. I don't know how to make up for this."

She moved quickly past my first suggestion but seized on my second, which was to compensate for the loss of my boiled carrots, watercress with vinegar, and Fig Newton bar by bringing me as much Jack Daniel's whiskey as I could put away in the remaining hour and a half. Pleased as hell that she had managed to repair some customer damage (not to mention avoiding caving in to my first suggestion for atonement), she scampered off and returned with three beautiful filets and five little airplane bottles of Daniel's. She hovered as I polished off the steaks and whiskey, trying to make them come out even so I could save her a trip for seconds. She was appreciative, and like a flash was back with three more steaks and five more little

bottles of whiskey. Not being a pig, for dessert I had one filet and one little bottle of whiskey. By the time I got off that plane, I was not only happy, I wondered why, in the name of all that's holy, the airline had ever considered offering meals of anything else but all the steak you can eat and whiskey you can drink.

As if I weren't already in nirvana, as I left the plane, the stewardess thanked me for being understanding (about the missing salad, vegetable, and dessert, I guess) and slipped me four more little tickets good for drinks on my next flight with her airline. Which was in about half an hour, when I caught the second leg of my flight.

Now, I was already in a state of gratitude to the gods second only to that of the Israelites when the Red Sea closed in on Pharaoh's army, right? I got on the next flight and settled in. The moment we were in the air, the steward got on the intercom and announced, "Good evening, ladies and gentlemen. I have good news for you. This is one of our special two-fer flights, and in a moment, when I come down the aisle with the beverage cart, you can have two drinks for the price of one." And I had four tickets good for four drinks: 4 x 2 = 8. When I got home that night, I was carrying maybe 40 extra pounds of luggage, maybe ten of it filets, thirty of it whiskey. I drank out of those cute little airplane bottles for another week.

Not all specialties, on the other hand, are exercises in excess. One fellow I know nailed down what has to be the simplest specialty I've ever heard of, arguably the simplest possible: hasty pudding and frumenty, incredibly ancient foods that are little more than heated grain and water. Thing is, they're simple . . . and interesting. They are breakfast foods you can talk about, prepare anywhere, and are pretty good, actually. An unlikely advantage to this approach is that no one knows what frumenty and hasty pudding are supposed to taste like. You can do the same thing by bringing a bottle of Strega, a pan of mostacolli, or a hunk of Mexican goat cheese. When the Pilgrims came to America and started stealing food from the Indians (they did), they said they didn't like corn. For one thing, it wasn't the corn they were used to. They called wheat and barley and rye corn. This was maize. Different stuff altogether. But they couldn't help comparing it with what they already knew and liked, and they didn't like the comparison at all. On the other hand, they had never eaten pumpkin, but they liked it fine, because they hadn't eaten anything like it. Nothing to compare it with. So it was fine.

If you show up somewhere with what you advertise to be a preparation just like McDonald's Chicken McNuggets, everyone is going to be disappointed. It isn't just like McDonald's Chicken McNuggets. You're not fooling anyone. I know McDonald's Chicken McNuggets, and these aren't McDonald's Chicken McNuggets. On the other hand, if you whip up some hasty pudding or frumenty, maybe they'll like it, and maybe they won't, but they sure as hell won't be disappointed because it isn't just like Mom's hasty pudding or frumenty.

Hasty Pudding and Frumenty

Cutting terminology closely and labeling "food"
those things you can eat without preparation, and

"dishes" foods you have to "fix," hasty pudding and frumenty have to be the simplest dishes ever devised by man. They are ancient and primal. Frumenty is known worldwide and is probably the first grain dish ever eaten, other than chomping raw seeds. We're talking caveman stuff here. Maybe the same could be said of hasty pudding, but since it is made of New World maize, it didn't find its way into European and Anglo-American culture until about an hour and a half after Columbus landed on the continent. Again, I suspect it's one of the first, if not the very first way maize corn was prepared for human consumption other than raw or roasted on the cob.

Frumenty is, at its most basic, raw wheat soaked overnight in water. And that's it. Then you eat it. It can be heated, mixed with raisins, sweet syrups, jellies or jams, honey, milk, sugar, brown sugar, anything you would normally put on a cereal, but it remains, at its heart, soggy wheat. The grain softens, swells, disintegrates, and gets gelatinous. I know it sounds terrible, but it is really quite tasty and very filling. I have talked with many people who remember their pioneer parents or grandparents eating this most fundamental of cereals every morning of every day of their lives. These days, when crushed wheat or corn or oats carries the price tag of the finest filets, why not enchant your children—or yourself—with something neolithic in its history, yummy, and ridiculously cheap? You can buy a bushel of wheat, a year's supply of frumenty, for what you'll pay in the store for four ounces of Fluffy Frosted Wheat Treats.

Simply take a quarter or half cup of raw wheat kernels. Soak them in plenty of water. They soak up and swell like beans. The next morning, do what you want by way of heating or eating, fancying or flavoring. Then eat the stuff. I can't imagine anything more organic. If you make this a specialty food, think how simple it will be to amaze your hosts with this primal breakfast. Hell, you can carry the ingredients in your pocket.

Hasty pudding isn't much more, except that it's made out of cornmeal, and can be even quicker—thus "hasty." Take cornmeal, mix it slowly into a half saucepan of boiling water until it is a loose slurry, pour it into a hot, greased pan like pancake batter, let it heat until it sets up and turns brownish on the bottom, and scramble it around until the whole mess is hot and browned. You can make the stuff a little more solid by adding egg, milk, and some salt, even a little wheat flour, but that sort of spoils the idea, doesn't it? I know a guy who uses this for his camp breakfasts. It requires virtually no supplies other than cornmeal, which you can also use to coat fish or meat for supper. Like frumenty, hasty pudding can be served with syrup, raisins, nuts, whatever.

You can also expand a bit on the process and make mush. Use a pot rather than a pan, although you can do this in a frying pan too, especially if you have some sort of cover. Mix up the meal and water, adding meal slowly to boiling water and a little salt. Cook for a couple minutes and take from fire. Cookbooks like *The Joy of Cooking* recommend using a double boiler, but I'm presuming that, as a man, you're not really prepared to mess up two pots for one simple dish. I'm also presuming you're going to use my good advice and get yourself some good cast iron, which will eliminate most situations where you need a double boiler anyway. So, take your cast iron pot with the mush in it from the fire. It'll stay hot while you continue to stir it for a few more minutes, until the mess gets real gooey.

It's been a while, but at this point I used to let the mush cool, in a few minutes when I was camping in cold weather, or overnight during warmer seasons. The mush sets up and can be sliced then and fried in a hot, buttered pan, giving it a crispy crust and nutty taste. This stuff is really good. I like it with maple syrup.

It's not necessary that you *manufacture* your specialty. Dan Selden has tons of little dry sausages made when he has his annual deer processed, and after hunting season, he comes around to all his friends, doling out packages of the zesty meat. He doesn't exactly *make* the sausage, but it's *his*. There used to be a popcorn factory in my little rural town, and wherever I went, I carried five-pound bags of gourmet popcorn with me as gifts. A friend from Arizona has found a small commercial operation—actually a Mexican family working in their garage—that makes exquisite salsa and hot sauce. He buys the stuff by the case at rock-bottom prices and hands it out like business cards. That's his specialty. "Big Jim"—"hot sauce"—the concepts as inseparable as right and left gloves (except of course in Brentwood).

LIBATIONS

Drink no longer water, but use a little wine for thy stomach's sake.

> —First Epistle of Paul the Apostle
> to Timothy

Oh, many a peer of England brews
Livelier liquor than the Muse,
And malt does more than Milton can
To justify God's ways to man . . .

> —A. E. Housman,
> *A Shropshire Lad*, 1896

Eat, drink, and be merry, for tomorrow you may be in Utah.

> —Linda's T-shirt

THINK OF IT AS MEDICINE—

A few pages ago I mentioned that the Pilgrims drank beer and a lot of it. That was because they didn't have much luck growing wheat or rye on the sandy soils of Cape Cod and therefore had too little bread. What is beer but liquid bread—

grain, yeast, a little sweetening, a dash of salt? Beer is good stuff, especially the way the Pilgrims drank it, young and green, full of yeast, rich in vitamin B, green bitters, rich in vitamin C, to offset the sweet malts, rich in carbohydrates and sugars. More and more of the advantages of wines are being discovered in the world's laboratories—one current discovery, for example, is that red wines in particular but wine in general (and FLASH: the latest evidence that dark beers, too) dramatically reduce problems of heart disease. Whiskey, gin, vodka are . . . can . . . well, they must be good for something or God wouldn't have given them to us.

By the way, the Pilgrims loved their gin, too, importing it from Holland by the barrel, and when their apple trees finally started bearing . . . aha! hard cider!! Remember that the next time you're at Grandma's for Thanksgiving and she makes some comment about putting the Pilgrims back in Thanksgiving. As if that weren't enough, know what the Pilgrims did on Thanksgiving after they ate? They watched a football game. No, I am not joking. That is precisely what they did. If you don't believe me, check with the folks at Plimoth Plantation's Pilgrim village.

And while they were watching that game, they were drinking beer—a heavy, dark beer like English beers or the stouts being turned out by more and more small breweries across America these days. The Pilgrims saw no particular connection between their intense religious dedication and the enjoyment of drink, other than that God is indeed good. I don't know where the notion that links alcohol, a gift from God if there ever were one, with the goofy notion that Jesus drank Nehi grape pop at the Last Supper came from. But let's discard it immediately from our discussions and make a point next Thanksgiving to remember our Pilgrim forefathers as they would want to be remembered, with a couple dry martinis before supper and plenty of Guinness stout to wash down the turkey.

Which is not to say you have to drink alcohol. You just have to mind your own business and not decide for others what they may or may not do. My son and one daughter don't drink. My Linda drinks very little. My best friend doesn't drink—and he runs a tavern. Every once in a while I will take a long schluck from a glass of our well water, and I am surprised all over again how good it is, straight from the ground beneath our feet. There are also a lot of bottled waters that seem particularly good. ("Taste" doesn't seem to be a word that fits well with what water is supposed to do.) I like water with a drop or two of lime or lemon juice in it. I like lemonade. All of those things strike me as good things to drink with food.

My modest cellar boasts some fancier beers—I like to keep on hand some Guinness as a stout and Newcastle Brown Ale for a dark beer. I keep some Pilsner Urquell for a pilsner, Harp as a lager, Bass's India Pale Ale, and some microbrewery products for interest and variety. (Beer won't keep all that long, especially the ones from microbreweries, so there's no sense in trying to keep a big inventory around for a protracted period.) Then I have what we call our utility beer. I like Budweiser, preferring the bottle to the can, but I don't mind moving around a little, either. I'll try this beer if it's cheap, or that beer if it sounds interesting. Sometimes I'll just get a hunger for the raw peanut taste of a cheap malt liquor like Colt .45, or a thirst for the watery nothingness of Coors. So I drink it. I've never been fond of nonalcoholic beers, but we always keep some around for Linda, or my folks, or any other nondrinkers who show up at the door. Just as I don't consider drinking to be a denial of God, neither is abstinence a breach of faith. The last drink I had was six months ago; the next one will taste all the better for the hiatus.

Wine's another matter when it comes to longevity. It won't last forever on the shelf, but it does better than beer. I keep a goodly stock of reds and whites, mostly dry, mostly American, mostly cheap enough to enjoy rather than to horde as an investment. Just as I do with food, I'll try anything in the way of wines. I love retsina, the resinous wine of Greece, which for all the world tastes like turpentine. I once pulled a nasty gag on a friend with retsina. He said how much he liked it, so I brought a bottle. He had to run off somewhere and do something, during which time I drank all the retsina. I knew he'd want some, so I filled the bottle with white vinegar. He drank it and didn't notice the difference. I'm not looking down my nose at him. He could have done the same thing to me with kerosene or turpentine.

I have a couple ports and sherries for predinner sips or desserts—my favorite dessert in this world is port with Stilton cheese, some English walnuts, and a pear or apple. Wow. In fact, cheese and fruit and just about any kind of wine is the best dessert I can imagine. Gouda and a Sauternes, feta and sherry. Oh, yum!! Linda and I were once on a cruise and had choices of the most voluptuous, rich desserts you can imagine, from flaming this to cognacked that. Me, I took port and Stilton, some nuts and a fruit. Can't beat it.

In fact, cheese is an important element in any man's cooking, because (1) it doesn't need anything done to it to be good, (2) it can be eaten with the fingers, and (3) the best of it smells the worst, a kind of male metaphor. Right now I'm enchanted with a terrific Mexican goat cheese a small bodega in Grand Island carries; it is an inexpensive, dryish, white cheese, fragrant but not pungent, and . . . it makes my mouth water just to think of it. Why buy that hideous American cheeselike, almost dairy product when you can get a real taste experience for not much more money? I can't imagine.

All this imported cheese and port wine talk may sound pretty highfalutin to some of you clods, but it isn't. My favorite port is Whidbeys, made in Washington State and fairly painless for the budget. And Stilton is so rich a cheese that you can't eat much of it no matter how much you like it, so even though it's expensive, you won't need much to satisfy your hunger for elegance. One trick for eating exotic is to avoid the gourmet sections of large grocery stores . . . but make a point of finding little groceries, bodegas, rice shops, whatever in the ethnic parts of your larger towns. Grand Island, Nebraska, is the closest thing to us by way of a real town—maybe 35,000 people—but even it has a small Southeast Asian part of town, and an increasingly large Latino section. And those folks like their food, and they may not find it at the Bag 'n' Save, so they have little shops of their own. And we get to go there, too! They're nice people, and their food is terrific—bread, sauces, meats, cheese, canned goods, all cheap and interesting, if not always to my taste. But I try everything.

I can't recall the first time I tasted kimchi, but I do remember the first time I heard of it. I was an apple-cheeked lad just starting my seven-year military obligation with the National Guard, the same week the older guys were coming back from Korea. With stories of kimchi, allegedly a relish that is buried in a clay pot for long periods of time before it is eaten. All I know is that it is hot, delicious, and looks as if it's made with cabbage or lettuce and lots of other salady sorts of things. I take two pieces of toast, butter them lightly, put in a thick layer of kimchi, and call it lunch. God, I love the stuff.

It's fermented, and what's wacky is that even in my fridge the stuff continues to bubble and toot (and, for that matter, in my gut for two days after ingestion). The folks at the Oriental grocery think it's great that a round-eyes comes in to buy their stuff and praises it to high heaven, and I think it's great to get delicious and interesting food cheaply. So we're all happy.

When I lived in Lincoln, I regularly stopped in at an Arabic shop, a Vietnamese grocery, and a German bakery. Snoop around. I'll bet you can find something like that not far from you.

But we were talking about drink. People I admire most when it comes to food, like Jay Anderson or Jim Harrison, don't look for the best of wherever they are. They look for the most typical. Drink what the locals drink. Find out what's made here in town, or just over the hill. You can get Budweiser anywhere. While you're here, why not try Auld Roger's Skullpopper? For one thing, if you do this, you're going to make some friends. You may be a stranger, but if you're drinking what the local boys are drinking, well then, you must be all right. Ask the barkeep or waiter or cook. Or better yet, ask one of the customers. You know, you walk into this little tavern in a little town and it's obvious to everyone you're a stranger. Conversation dies and everyone looks you over. "What'll you have?" the man asks.

You look over the mugs of reddish brew in front of the guys sitting playing cards at the next table. "I'll have some of that," you say.

"Then you want a red one?" he asks.

"Sure. If it's good enough for those fellows, it should be good enough for me. What exactly is a 'red one'?"

"Why, that's the way we drink beer around here in the morning—a cold mug with a little tomato juice in it."

And that's the way it is around here, too. And it's not bad.

Red Beer

Actually, this isn't as goofy as it sounds. In Germany, *Bier mit Tschuss,* beer with a squirt of fruit juice, is a breakfast standard. I used to love a Chinese beer called Sweet China, which had a generous dollop of pineapple juice in it. Red beer is simply tap beer or bottled or canned beer with tomato juice added to taste. You can go into a lot of rural taverns in Nebraska asking for a beer and get the response, "Plain?" Of course visitors are stumped, because they don't know what the alternative is. Plain as opposed to what?! In many parts of rural America, the alternatve is red beer. Locals around here have their own recipes—beer with tomato juice but also an added ingredient: celery salt, season salt, Tabasco sauce, Worcestershire sauce. Others prefer V8. I like mine with regular bar stock Bloody Mary mix. Yum-yum.

WHEN IN DEUTSCHLAND

Drinking in strange places requires some diplomacy, especially when you're traveling alone, especially when you're in another culture where things are likely to be done differently from the way they are at home. I once visited a tiny town in a remote area of Germany because outside this crossroads (literally) there was a mountain on the map labeled Welschberg. Welsch Mountain. Wow. That would be a nice thing to have in my memory bank: the day I scaled the north face of Welsch Mountain. So I went to this little town. And I climbed Welsch

Mountain, which was for all the world like climbing one or two flights of stairs. Didn't amount to much. But I had already checked into a room above the local tavern, so I rappelled back down the mountain—just kidding!—and strolled into the tavern. This was early

on a Saturday afternoon. A bunch of guys, clearly laborers and farmers from their dress, were sitting at a big table and they had obviously been putting away a few brews. I said hello (I spoke German fairly well at the time) and went to another table.

There was the silence and the stares and the innkeeper asked what I wanted to drink. I said a beer, a local beer, and he brought it to me. The guys at the other table started talking again, but there was, even at a distance, an unpleasant tone to their conversation. And they kept looking over at me with distinctly unfriendly expressions. Finally one of the more sloshed good ol' boys got up, hitched up his britches and came strolling—well, it was more like weaving—toward my table.

Oh-oh. This didn't look good. He said, in German, "You're too good for workmen and farmers, then, I suppose?"

"No," I said, "I'm just visiting from America, wanted a beer, and didn't want to interrupt you fellows since I'm a stranger here."

Well, everything fell apart at that point. The guy was thoroughly chagrined. He had thought I was an uppity Kraut, maybe from a city somewhere since my German was kind of schoolish. He had no idea I was a visitor from America. Thing is, he explained, around here, when you come into a tavern, you're supposed to sit down with whoever is there already. He had worked for Americans after the Big War and he understood how goofy we are about all wanting separate tables. Now that I knew the way things are supposed to be done, he insisted, I had to join them.

I didn't have to pay for a beer the rest of the day. They hauled me along to an Old Boys soccer game they were playing in (in soccer an Old Boy is anyone over thirty years old), and then we drank a keg of local suds after the game. The older fellow who had befriended me walked me around the countryside visiting and seeing sights until well after midnight, when we finally came rolling back into town. (We were walking, but we were rolling.)

As we walked down the hill toward the single streetlight at the one intersection of the village, I could see coming from the other direction a short, stout woman, walking up that hill with an unmistakable air of determination about her. He told me, but he didn't have to: It was his wife. He had sort of forgotten that he was supposed to go home for supper before the soccer game, and probably should have gone home after the soccer game, and. . . . We stood there in the glare of that streetlight for a short but lively lecture from the little lady who looked for all the world like most of my German aunts, and the first moment she paused for a breath, maybe three minutes into her tirade, as quickly as he could, with a minimum of words, he told her I was (1) a professor, (2) lost, (3) from America, and (4) studying the traditions and history of the region—okay, it was a little exaggeration, but a harmless one.

Again, like one of my aunts, she turned from ogre into hostess at the wave of that only slightly fraudulent wand (I was a professor, and I was from America) and she would accept nothing less than that I come to her house for a late breakfast the next morning, and we were both off the hook, just like that.

On that same trip I was visiting the wine regions of the Mosel, Nahe, and Rhine valleys as a part of my long study of vintning (wine making). (That was the story I told *my* wife.) I did know quite a bit, and I found that you don't need to know a lot to be an exceptional American in the eyes of most of the world. Americans have the reputation of being ignorant slobs or arrogant boors, which, if you think about it, really does take in damn near every American you can think of. So the goal is to strike somewhere in the middle of all that. Know enough that you can speak with some intelligence about something, but be sure you understand not only how much you know, but also how little you know. For nearly a year before I went on this trip, I read everything I could about the wines of the regions I was visiting. I knew those valleys vineyard by vineyard. I tried to learn the German vocabulary of wine. I planned my trip carefully. I traveled by bicycle, but I'm no cycler, so I figured on traveling only a few hours each morning.

Why not just rent a car and drive slowly? In Germany that borders on suicidal. I've never seen such utter idiots when it comes to driving. Say you are in a Volkswagen and cruising along about sixty miles an hour on the Autobahn—where there is, by the way, no speed limit. In your rearview mirror you see a car coming up behind you, and then, just like that, it *is* behind you. It's a Mercedes-Benz and he's doing, oh, maybe 120 miles an hour. You are in his way, and there is a car in the other lane. What do you suppose that driver is going to do? I'll tell you what he's going to do, because I've seen it done—he'll bump you from behind to give you some inclination to get out of his way. Maybe you'll be especially accommodating and just roll your car into the ditch, where it will explode and burn. I've seen that, too.

Believe me, unless you're an idiot, you won't want to drive in Germany, especially if you intend to take your time.

Germany is not a big place to begin with, however, and I was covering only a small part of it, so I could take my time. I probably could have walked. Next time, I'll take local buses and trains. Insofar as possible I made room reservations well in advance—in small towns wherever possible, on back roads, in castles, in places I'd read about, places with good vineyards. Sometimes I stayed at inns associated with the vineyards themselves. So I'd take off in the morning, stop and look at some vineyards, maybe stop at a winery I'd read about, I'd order a glass of an ordinary wine from that winery, and ask some questions. These people are small farmers; the folks who make the wine are the ones who sell it, pretty much out of their parlors. First, the Germans were impressed that I spoke German, and knew some of the language of wine. And they were amazed that I knew about wine itself, and that I was asking questions and listening to the answers. "Come here," they'd say. "I want to show you something in the cellar." And down we'd go into medieval, maybe Roman-built caverns, where thousands of bottles of wine were coolly maturing. "If you like what we're selling upstairs, try this."

And pretty soon we would be surrounded by open, half-empty bottles, laughing, drinking, talking. The doorbell would ring as some other traveler stopped by for a cool glass of white wine. "Never mind," my host would laugh. "There will be another," and he'd pop another cork. Late afternoon I'd wheel into another town and the process would start all over. It was a postgraduate education in German wine, and it was all there for the price of spending the time to get to know a little and giving up the fiction of knowing it all.

Strangers in strange places also need to know enough not to drink too much or, for that matter, drink at all. I am very close to several Native American communities, and I know and understand their sensitivity to alcohol and its ravages. I never

drink on a reservation or with Native American friends. It's not only a cultural gaffe, it's dangerous. That could be a racist thing to say, but I'm not the one who said it. An Indian friend said it to me not long after he almost killed two people during a drinking bout. He liked me, so he gave me good advice: "Roger, don't drink with me." But I'm German. My people have been drinking alcohol for two thousand years, at least, usually before going into battle, in contrast to Indians, who have been using alcohol a couple centuries at the most. I am the result of two millennia of accelerated natural selection, fitted and suited to consuming alcohol—and a lot of it. My capacity is notable. Not Indians. For them it can be pure poison. (There are also a lot of social, psychological, and cultural factors within the problem Indians have with alcohol, but I'll have that for another book.)

WHEN IN GEORDIE LAND

I was once in Newcastle, England, for a bunch of reasons. I wanted to visit old friends John and Muriel Wishart, and I even then loved Newcastle Brown Ale. Newcastle Brown has a nasty reputation; legend has it that there is a special ward of the Newcastle Hospital devoted entirely to those who drink the Brown. How's that for a reputation?! A bunch of things happened on that visit that I've never forgotten. For one thing, John, I found, made a habit of going up to his club (pronounced "cloob") every evening about nine to gossip with his cronies for an hour until the cloob closed at 10:15, by the Queen's law. Then he'd come home where Muriel had fixed a little hot snack, maybe pasties (pronounced PASS-tees, a lovely hot pie), for him before he retired. I recall, in fact, one evening at John's cloob, when a completely smashed buddy of John's asked me what time it was. I looked at my watch and said, "Nine-thirty." "Oh, God, I wish it were ten-fifteen," he said, "so I could go home!"

I'm not sure I understood the implications of that conversation until the next night when John announced he'd decided to forgo his nightly visit to the cloob and we would instead sit at home and chat in his parlor. Muriel exploded, to the astonishment of all of us, including John, and maybe Muriel. "Now, you look here, John Wishart. This is the only hour of the day I have to myself in this house, when I can do as I like, and not have to look after you. You just pack up and get yourself up to the cloob and drink your beer." Obediently, we packed up and left. It seemed the only right thing to do.

There were more surprises at the cloob. The folks in this northernmost area of England are called Geordies, and their English is not what you learned in school, believe me. I could barely understand it. This one fellow talked to me and talked to me, but I couldn't understand a word he was saying. Finally John interpreted for me, "He says he wants to know about your travels." I explained I was going to be around here a little while and then would be leaving for Wales, to the southwest of England, clear across the island. The man launched into a long, spirited lecture about something, of which I understood absolutely not a word. After fifteen minutes of this, I turned to John again, seeking linguistic help. John listened, laughed, and then reported, "He says it's going to be tough for you in Wales. They don't speak decent English like us. You won't be able to understand a word they say."

But we were talking about beer, right? I'll get back to that in a second, but first I have to talk about size and beer. I don't know the physiology of the matter, but I'd guess big people can handle more alcohol than little people. At least that's my experience. Geordies tend to be small folks; I'm a big fella. A Geordie rugby team, no wienies, walked into the cloob about the time I got up to get another beer and they stopped dead in their tracks in admiration of my bulk.

"How many stone do you weigh?" one asked. "You're as big as the bloody door!"

As is my custom in situations like this where there is so much to learn, I decided to sample everything I could, not realizing that in many parts of the world, certainly in Newcastle, the old adage "Never mix, never worry" is not understood precisely as I take it. My impression is that one shouldn't mix, say, strawberry milkshakes and straight bourbon whiskey. (I still believe that *is* good advice.) So I ordered a Federation ale, then a stout, then a bitter, then a lager. Then a pint of Newcastle Brown, and a Watney's pilsner, and a Guinness stout. And then maybe a local hard cider.

In Newcastle, it turns out, they think it boggling to drink a Federation *ale* in the same evening as a Federation *bitter*. Before long I noticed even those who had grown accustomed to my bulk at the table were nonetheless watching me with growing interest. There was no hostility, not even curiosity, certainly no disapproval. They seemed ... interested. I finally had to ask John just what the hell was going on. He explained that they were waiting to see me fall, wanting to be on the event but not a part of it, as it were. They just could not believe that a human being was mixing potations like that and still standing. Well, *sitting*. A little after ten, when we left the club, a flattering round of applause followed us out the door. It was a fine moment. I think I also heard the strains of "The Star-Spangled Banner" playing as I circled the Olympic track in triumph.

WHEN IN NEBRASKA

I thoroughly enjoy single-malt Scotches. The first I ever tasted was that Glencoe Jay Anderson bought and drank out of Priscilla Alden's . . . er, the museum curator's shoe. Since then, maybe because of that, I am utterly enamored of those heavy, pricey whiskies. I also enjoy slivovitz, a Slavic plum brandy that is almost impossible to get in Nebraska anymore, which says nothing about the rest of the world. Whenever I go someplace like Mexico I pick up local favorites like mescal or tequila. I enjoy Southern Comfort and, as noted, Jack Daniel's green label. I keep some exotics like ouzo. I love Strega or a good brandy for dessert. I wish I could afford more.

There is something of the snob in me, I'll have to admit. I was once at the Cornhusker Hotel in Lincoln, a terrific, top-of-the-line place, having supper with a couple of very good friends, who happen to be state legislators. We had a good meal and were down to dessert, a specialty of the Cornhusker. We'd had a few bottles of wine, and I was savoring the moment I could pick up the check and stick the idiots who ran CBS with the bill. (I was doing legitimate business for CBS, but I knew how the asses who ran that outfit were thinking—they'd just as soon we ate braunschweiger and onion sandwiches while they slopped up caviar, drank French champagne, and laughed at those of us who were doing the work and making their parasitic livings for them. By the way, CBS is now under new management and may be on the rebound. I love my new bosses. I love my job. They're terrific. What great folks!)

Okay, I've regained my composure. It takes me a minute to bring myself back under control when I think about how those bloodsuckers destroyed the fantastic institution that was CBS. Anyway, it was one of many moments when I screwed those boys while they thought they were screwing me. The legislators who were going to be part of our story ordered their chocolate foofoos and moosey falafalas. I don't like sweet stuff, as you already know, so I looked over the after-dinner drink list. Wow. Grand Marnier. That sounds good—tart, sharp, clean, orange. Yeah, I'll have some of that.

"Twelve-year-old, twenty-five-year-old, or seventy-five-year-old, sir?" The waiter asked. Huh? Whoa!

"Uh, how much is the seventy-five-year-old?" (I know, I know: I blew my sophistication act when I asked. I should have just ordered the stuff, damn the price.)

"Thirty-two dollars a shot, sir."

My friends looked at me triumphantly. I know what they were thinking. "Dumb shit. He thought he'd get something fancy and impress us by rolling out nine dollars, and now here he is, down to two chips and it's his turn to ante."

"Fine," I said cheerfully. "Make it a double."

It was elegant, and I loved it, and thank you very much, Mr. Tisch, wherever you are.

The moral is, even if you can't afford much by way of something elegant, have something. Have something on hand that is there for only very special occasions, and then it isn't really all that expensive. One Christmas, Lovely Linda knocked me down as if a bowling ball had been dropped on my head. She has not always been extravagant or inventive when it comes to presents. That's okay, I'm not complaining. It's just a fact. So, one Christmas I opened a gift from her that was clearly a boxed bottle, and I thought, "Wow, that's neat, she got me a nice bottle of Scotch maybe, or a wine." I opened it. Holy bananas. I looked at the bottle. I looked at her, utterly bewildered. It was a bottle of the finest French champagne you could buy in Nebraska—$100 a bottle. And she had bought me a bottle. I was absolutely flabbergasted. I gushed, and my eyes teared up, and I was, for once, speechless. I would, I finally mumbled, save this bottle for something . . . something so spectacular . . . well, I couldn't imagine a situation where that bottle of exquisite wine would be appropriate. We'd probably never drink it. I would put it in my cellar and look at it and dream. Wow. Then she could maybe bury me with it. Thank you, Lovely Linda.

I opened the next present, and it was . . . O my God . . . another bottle of the same wine! She knew precisely what I would want to do—save the wine for a special occasion—but she wanted me to have the sublime pleasure of tasting that wine this Christmas, so she bought me a saving bottle and a drinking bottle. Fellas, if you find a woman who thinks like that, hang on to her.

WHEN IN GREENWICH VILLAGE

One more story about the importance of knowing a little bit about what you're doing when it comes to eating and drinking and then we'll move on to something else. Charles Kuralt is an old friend of mine. That's not bragging, it's simply the truth. When I visit him, we—Kuralt, his wife, and I—go to the same restaurant every time. He always protests that he wants to take me someplace really fancy and new and special, but this little walk-down Italian restaurant, the Beatrice, has become a favorite of mine, quite separate from its association with Charles.

The food is excellent and the people who run the place (including the cooks and waiters) are such superb human beings, it wouldn't matter if the food were pure crapola (the Italian word for . . . oh, never mind). Anyway, the first time we went to the Beatrice, maybe fifteen years ago, we enjoyed a great meal and time came for dessert. Everyone ordered something or another, but given that I'm not really fond of sweet foods, I thought I'd like an after-dinner drink. A brandy and Benedictine? No, that's a little too heavy. Galliano is also too sweet, and even a Strega seemed a bit much. I wanted something dry and clean, maybe . . . yes, that's it, I wanted a bit of grappa.

Grappa is peasant liquor. It's like moonshine. It is distilled from the leftover scraps of stems, grape skins, hulls, and seeds, whatever is left over in the wine presses after the wine has been pressed from them. You take all this leftover junk and toss it into a still and take off whatever alcohol is left and whatever is left of the perfume and esters and essences. Then the peasants drink it.

That's me. I like grappa. "Do you have any . . . grappa?" I asked. Grappa is not easy to find. It's easier to find really great stuff than it is to find really dreadful stuff when it comes to drink. Here I was in a top-notch fancy restaurant with a national television star and I ordered what amounts to Appalachian moonshine. Aldo Cardia, proprietor of the Beatrice, looked at me in disbelief. "You want . . . grappa?" he asked.

"Well, if you have any. I don't want to cause any trouble. Just if you have some, I think it would be a great end to a great meal, but don't. . . ."

Aldo turned to his wife, Elsie, and the head waiter, Marco:

"Mr. Welsch, he wants GRAPPA!" He threw up his hands as if in triumph. Elsie and Marco did, too. "He wants grappa. He must have *the* grappa."

"The" grappa? What is "the" grappa? Aldo disappeared and in a moment returned cradling a plain, clear-glass, unlabeled bottle in his arms. "*The* grappa," he explained, looking at it out of the side of his eyes. He held the bottle up for Elsie and Marco to admire.

"*The* grappa," they agreed.

He put a large, thick glass in front of me. And he poured me some—a glassful of *the* grappa. I sipped. It was exquisite. It was nectar. It was moonshine. It was smuggled. It was illegal. It was precious. It was *the* grappa, and no damned wonder. At 2 A.M., the Beatrice had been empty for hours. We sat with Aldo drinking that wonderful stuff while he talked about Italy, about his years in the Italian submarine service during World War Two, about food and drink, and about *the* grappa, who made it, how it was made, what it meant, what a rare thing it was to find someone who understood.

I don't know how many times I've visited the Beatrice since then, or how much of *the* grappa I've poured into this body, but it has never been anything but wonderful all over again. Then Aldo died. I knew he was older than me—a lot older than me, but you know how such things go. I wanted him to go on forever, and so I naturally assumed he would. But on my last visit, none of us expecting what was going to happen, as I left, he handed me two of the heavy, thick grappa glasses I associated with the magic moments I had spent with him. Then he did the unthinkable: He gave me a bottle—A BOTTLE—of *the* grappa. It was as if he had given a gift of his soul, a portion of himself, a share of his life. In my cellar that bottle sits in an honored place, along with the two glasses. Once, I can't even remember the occasion, I drank a thimble of it. Maybe I'll have some more again soon. I don't want to forget its taste and its meaning.

And that's what comes of knowing just a little about what counts and having the humility to ask for the rest. You don't get something like that out of a slice of carrot cake in a fern-infested yuppie salad bar.

TOOLS OF THE TRADE

Fingers were made before forks, and hands before knives.
—JONATHAN SWIFT,
Polite Conversation, 1738

Curlylocks, Curlylocks,
Wilt thou be mine?
Thou shalt not wash dishes
Nor yet feed the swine . . .
—ANONYMOUS

STICKS AND STONES

During my bachelor years, I, like so many other men in the same situation, brought the processes of food preparation and consumption pretty much down to a kind of time-motion efficiency exercise. I produced fewer dirty dishes in a week than my wife now generates in making a piece of toast. I cooked foods right in their cans, and then ate them from the can, resulting in one (1) dirty spoon or fork and one (1) discarded can. The same spoon or fork served double duty then while preparing the dog's meal. By the end of a typical evening, my sink would hold one (1) spoon or fork and one (1) glass. No sense in using a sink of hot water and soap for so little; it'll wait just fine until Saturday. Sometimes not even a week would fill that sink.

This is not a new idea. Plains pioneers rarely had anything more than an absolute minimum of cooking utensils. Children grew up not only knowing exactly what they had by way of eating tools like forks, but *recognizing those forks by their names!*

"Mom, here's Three Tine but I can't find Stubby."

"There he is, over by the stove, darling."

Billions of people eat with two sticks, including some who don't have to. Nothing suits me more than being in a party of diners at a Chinese restaurant when show-offs ask for chopsticks. They don't use them right—they pick up dainty morsels one at a time and convey them precariously from table to mouth, which is like trying to carry a bowling ball with two tenpins, instead of holding the food bowl up directly under the chin and using the sticks to shovel gobs of food directly into the mouth, the way the Chinese do. As a result, the meal takes forever. But not for me. I'm busy working with tools I understand very well, fork and spoon, putting away the mooshu pork, cashew chicken, and Szechuan beef by the bushel basketful. And when the evening's over, we split the bill evenly. Seems fair to me!

I have published a mess of books before this one, one of which is about antique tractor restoration. Actually, it's about tools and men and machine shops and wrenches and rust and solvent. Just like this one. Frankly, you probably could have learned everything you have in *this* book in *that* book. Repairing old tractors and cooking potatoes are, as fate would have it, remarkably akin. The best piece of advice in that book, and the best piece of advice in this book, is when you buy a tool, buy a good one. You can buy a piece-of-crap can opener that will last you maybe four cans—or four days—for two dollars, depending on just how much of a bachelor you are, or, for twenty dollars, you can buy a Zwilling can opener (not electric, for Pete's sake—you don't need an electric can opener, jeez) that you will leave to your grandchildren. I don't think that's a contest.

PANNING THE POTS

You don't need a lot of pots and pans, either. Don't fool around with aluminum, Kmart junk, plastic, nylon, crappy steel, dinky junk. Buy one, buy one at a time, and make it good.

I am not talking about eating utensils. You can eat with your fingers. I'm talking about cooking utensils. And at this point I have to thank my first wife, Marilyn. Throwing me out of our house for *her* transgressions (a nice touch, I can now recognize, and one I will elaborate on in greater detail in my next guide for men, a text dealing with the natural progression from tractors and foods: love and romance), she issued me, from my own possessions, two plates, two cups, two forks, two spoons, and two knives. My presumption even then was that her understanding was that the paradigm would be "one clean/one dirty" rather than "one for Roger/one for gorgeous consort." Ha!!

Anyway, you don't need a lot of tools to cook and eat, but you do need good tools to cook, and damn near nothing but your fingers to eat. And here's what you need: CAST IRON! Forget Teflon tin. Forget glass. Forget plastic and aluminum. Get yourself a good cast-iron frying pan, a good cast-iron pot, and a Dutch oven. So much for pots. Your great-grandchildren will be using them! Food doesn't stick to cast iron. If it does, heat up the iron and burn it off. What the hell. It's iron.

The secret to cast iron is seasoning, which in the case of cast iron is not salt and pepper. Cast iron needs a bonded layer of cooking oil on it. You can't wash cast iron in soap and water or you'll remove that layer and destroy its principal advantage. So don't wash cast iron. Wipe it off. Since you have only three cooking vessels, you'll be using it again tomorrow. Forget all the crap about germs. They'll die. Heat your cast iron up when you buy it, very hot. Pour good cooking oil in it. Heat the living hell out of it. Cool it down. It's seasoned. Now, don't wash it. Wipe it out. If some idiot does wash it out, reseason it. Pass it on to your heirs.

Now, in all honesty, I also have some huge stainless steel pots for my summer kitchen, but if I could find a good three- or five-gallon cast-iron pot for the kitchen—one I could pick up—I'd use it. In the meantime, I need something to boil big hams and messes of ribs in, so I do have some big stainless.

For my grill and fireplace I have some great tools made by a local topnotch blacksmith, Jim Pepperl. I'll pass them along to my grandchildren. I think he gave them to us when we got married. When you get married, tell your relatives you're registered with the local blacksmith.

All you need is one or two good knives, and you won't find them in a store that sells cooking utensils. Go to a sporting goods store, or a sporting goods catalog, and buy real knives. Of course, buck knives are the best. Boom John gave me a buck knife once, and it was stolen in a burglary. What the ass who stole it doesn't know is that my name is engraved on the *back* spine of the blade. I have this dream in which I am somewhere with one of the creeps I suspect of the burglary, and we pull out some venison sausage for lunch, and he cuts into it with . . . a buck knife. I take the knife to cut the sausage and turn it over. I find my name on the spine and . . . whoops! The knife slips, and I cut the tendons on the backs of both his ankles. Oh shoot. He'll be crippled the rest of his life. Gosh, I hope his insurance premiums are up-to-date. In the meantime, I'll take my knife. Here's my name, right on the spine.

Buy yourself a good knife that will last forever, unless someone steals it: a Henckels Zwilling knife from Germany, for example. "Zwilling" means "twins," so the symbol on Henckels's knives is a stylized drawing of twins.

On the other hand, I like wooden spoons, pasta rakes, stirrers, that sort of thing. I'm suspicious of metal and food, but not of wood. And I'm not talking about hygiene. In fact, don't talk to me about hygiene. I am alive today because millions, maybe billions, of weaker wimps died when their puny bodies couldn't handle the pathogens, germs, viruses, bugs, filth, pollution, and all the other things they ate. What was left was Iron Gut Men like me. I am not about to defy natural selection and throw myself in the way of genetic progress. I will use wooden spoons: amoebas be damned.

I live in terror of the handle eventually falling off my coffeepot. After all these years, you'd think we'd have boiled everything down, you should excuse the expression, to the perfect pot—which is to say, mine. But no, you can't even find a pot like mine anymore. It looks like something out of a bad science lab: two huge silver balls, one on top of the other. The bottom is where the coffee winds up and has a handle and a spout, so we pour our coffee from it. The top ball has a little basket in its bottom, into which you put the coffee grounds, and a little perforated lid with a tall handle you stuff down on top of the basket so the grounds don't float around when you pour the hot water in. And that's it.

The pot's secret—and the secret of good coffee—is that the coffee itself is never boiled. You can't boil coffee without making it taste absolutely wretched. So there are still millions of Americans who use coffee percolators, which operate on the basis of boiling the

coffee. Man, is that stupid or what?! If nothing else, just get a big coffee kettle, throw a handful of grounds in it, pour boiling water over it, and strain the stuff as you pour it. That's better than a percolator, even if it is a little messy. (You can settle coffee grounds in camp coffee by tossing in a couple eggshells. It's a protein and ions thing. A cup of cold water tossed into the pot will also work.) A large lab beaker or carafe, a funnel, and disposable coffee filters make up about the most basic, inexpensive, thoroughly functional coffee maker you can put together.

Andy Rooney, a colleague and friend at CBS News, has gone one further step—in fact, a giant step—toward improving on this system. He boils water and places the grounds directly into the water rather than pouring the water over the grounds. This allows something more than erratic, momentary contact twixt grounds and water. Then Andy pours the water/grounds mixture through a filter in a filter funnel—I use filters in an ordinary kitchen sieve, which is a trifle faster, I think, than a solid funnel.

Another friend uses ordinary brown paper bathroom towels he steals from work; they are pure cellulose and tasteless and seem to work just as well as expensive commercial filters. Since I don't have a job, I have no place to steal paper towels, however. But I have stolen Andy Rooney's coffee process.

FOR EATIN' OFF'N

I have a curious ambivalence for tableware, "silver," plates, cups, glasses, and that sort of thing that I won't even try to explain. On the one hand, I don't think such things matter. The Pilgrims ate off boards and bread crusts, and that works for me. I like paper plates during the winter because (1) you wind up with fewer dishes to wash and (2) you toss the paper into the fireplace, thus recycling the paper, and contribute to the heating of the house. This is the one place I admire chopsticks. Without the civilizing influence of my wife, I'd still eat out of cans and focus my cuisine on finger foods. I bought some beer glasses from my favorite eatery-drinkery when it was going out of business a decade ago, and I like to drink out of them because of the memories. Linda insists on matched plates, but we are largely content with wildly assorted glasses and coffee mugs, mostly gifts or souvenirs—the emotional dimension of eating once again clearly more important than nutrition or taste, convenience or cost. Our wineglasses are cheap, tulip-shaped clunks I bought through the local barkeep, although again I do have my favorites—a short, squat, squarish glass I like for single malts and bourbon, a delicate wineglass that belonged to my folks and from which cheap wine seems to taste better, a glass I like for mixed drinks, a ceramic mug for cold beer, a couple little wineglasses (which I accidentally dropped in my hand luggage during an United flight) for liqueurs, and those two grappa glasses. I'm not motivated at all by a sense of elegance, but I like to drink even the cheapest utility beer from a glass rather than the bottle or can. I like to look at it, consider its color and head and bubbles, and then slug it down!

On the other hand, somewhere along the line, maybe fifteen years ago, I bought a beautiful, large burgundy glass with a delicate, fine stem and a clear tone when thumped on the rim. It holds a full half bottle of wine without crowding. Thing is, that one glass spoiled me. It is not only pretty, it not only shows off the wine and its perfume to their best advantage, it *feels* good in my fingers. I dread ever eating with a solid silver fork and spoon because the same thing might happen. And I get the feeling I am paying appropriate homage to good wines when I pour them into good crystal.

So I do. A few years ago I treated myself to a half dozen relatively expensive, big burgundy glasses like the big one I picked up at the garage sale, and a half-dozen tall, slim champagne flutes. (Those flattish bowls some places use for champagne are all wrong; what you want with good champagne, even decent champagne, is a tall, slender tube that shows off the bubbles.) You can buy the best glasses for a hundred dollars a pop, but that's way beyond my courage, never mind my budget; the sets of crystal I bought from a fancy catalog cost about eight dollars a glass—roughly fifty dollars for the set. I don't need something like that. I'd say it's vanity, but I rarely let any of my cloddish friends or relatives drink from them, so it's not simply a matter of showing off. They're mine. I enjoy them by myself, or with Linda. They make me feel good, and I can't think of a better reason to spend a little extra money. I drink from them only when we are springing for a special wine, so the glasses are not often in jeopardy. They'll last for years and years and years. Suddenly fifty dollars doesn't seem like all that much, does it?

FEELIN' GOOD

Now let's get down to the basic tools of male cuisine—fingers. Most people will tell you that they eat finger food because they're in a hurry, and it's convenient to hold the stuff in your hand while you continue driving on down the road, eating between stop signs. As usual, I think it's more than that. We like to look at food, we like to taste food, we like to smell food, WE LIKE TO FEEL FOOD!! While the epicures lament the decline, maybe disintegration—even perversion—of American foods as we more and more depart from dining and take up scarfing, I am encouraged, at least, by the fact that more and more Americans are abandoning the alienating tools of silverware and stuffing food into their mouths with their fingers.

And all you have to do is look around you to see that this trend has pretty much taken over American foodways—pizza, tacos, hot dogs, hamburgers, french fries, onion rings, gyros, heros, submarines, hot wings, kebabs, ice-cream cones, pineapple whips, candy bars, hors d'oeuvres, canapés, sushi, fried chicken, chip dips, popcorn, potato chips, corn chips, pork rinds, boiled eggs, sausages, *runzas*, *kolaches*, doughnuts, knishes, fried cheese, popcorn shrimp, on and on. Who would have thought, a couple years ago, that we would be eating a breakfast of eggs, sausage, and hash browns—with our fingers?!

Yes, there's an elegance to the formal table, but the fingers are not without their message, mostly one of primal simplicity. When our daughter Antonia was born, I wound up leaving her and Linda at the hospital and coming home very early in the morning—as I recall, about 4 A.M. I hadn't eaten for a day, I was exhausted, I was elated, I was relieved, I was vibrant and excited by the day's reminder of the processes of life. So, what to eat?

There was no other choice: good beef and good champagne. I got coals going quickly in the grill, dug out a couple of the best filets I could find in the freezer, defrosted them in the microwave, popped the corks on two bottles of champagne (once opened, there is nothing to do with champagne but drink it, and I didn't want to short myself on this celebration!), and lay back in the hammock to watch the stars in the clear sky, to think, to rejoice. When the fire was roughly right, I tossed the meat on the grill. It smelled wonderful. My mind was reeling with the thoughts of the day before—and the decades to come. Not only had I assisted at the birth of my daughter hours before, but two days before I had also assisted at the delivery of my first grandchild, in the same hospital room!

It just didn't make sense to stand around in the bright light of the kitchen, putting together a plate and service, a glass, napkins . . . all that. When the meat was ready—I like my beef rare, so it didn't take long—I pulled it from the grill with a long, iron cooking fork. And I ate it. I held it in my fingers while the juice ran down to my elbows and off my chins. I bit off juicy chunks, washing it down with good champagne from the bottle. I'm not an elegant fellow, maybe even something of a slob, but my purpose that morning was not to revel in degenerate behavior. Somehow, the unadorned simplicity of eating that way seemed precisely right at that moment. I probably should have done it naked. There are times for that sort of thing, too. Or maybe I should have eaten the meat raw. I always order my beef rare—the rarer the better. At my bachelor party, Boom John Carter asked me how I'd like my steak. I gave him my usual response, and he plunked the raw steak on my plate, right then and there. And I ate it. It was delicious.

GOING HIGH-TECH

Okay, after all that simplicity talk, there is one product from the most modern technology of food preparation that I most heartily applaud. But I sure didn't to begin with. I was having lunch with a New York lawyer, and he was curious about life on the central Plains. We talked about food, among other things, and I said that we have access to pretty much the same things he has in New York, and some things he doesn't—good beef, for example, and fresh produce direct from the fields. "The only thing I really miss in a small town like Dannebrog, Nebraska," I said, "is good bread. Mostly what we have is that pasty white crap that doesn't even deserve the label 'bread.'"

"Well, that's easily fixed," he said. "Get yourself a bread machine. We have one and couldn't live without it. We have fresh bread in the morning when we get up, or ready for slicing when we get home from work. Anything—sourdough, French bread, whole wheat, raisin bread . . . anything."

Thing is, I didn't quite understand what a bread machine does. It does everything. You put in water, bread mix, and yeast, set a timer, and a loaf of hot, fresh, crusty bread is ready to be sliced whenever you say the word. It's a kitchen miracle. It's a man's dream—eating without cooking. For that matter, cooking without cooking. Unless I lived above a French bakery, I cannot imagine living now without a bread machine. They're not cheap—I think they run around $150 these days—but if you enjoy eating, they pay for themselves in a matter of weeks. But forget economy when it comes to this kitchen item: think of it as you would a lava lamp or scented candle, as a simple giver of pleasure, aside from practicality. Because that's what it can be. Nothing—nothing!—perfumes a house like the smell of bread baking in the late afternoon. Man, that aroma lets everything fall into place. Simplicity for man food, yes, but I say, "Give us this day our daily bread machine."

Another device along much the same line is the Crock-Pot, the bachelor's friend, the cook without fear of alimony, the little brown jug. It may be possible to make a good food that isn't good in a Crock-Pot, but I haven't found it yet. Maybe ice cream. Surely you know about the Crock-Pot. It cooks long and slow and rarely has anything more complicated by way of controls than a switch that says "high" and "low." You set it on the counter of your kitchen (or the floor, if you are a bachelor), and you throw a bunch of stuff in it and some water or

juice of some kind or beer, and you turn it on and go away. When you come back, you have food. Good food. Try to hire a cook who'll do that for you.

I know it seems dreadfully inconsistent with my insistence on simplicity in male cookery and eatery, but I recommend a microwave. Your confusion here is a matter of cultural complexity rather than my own intellectual conflicts. The pioneer life was not a simple life; it was dreadfully complex. Not only did you do all your own cooking, you grew all your own food. You delivered your babies, and your horses'. You made your own furniture and own fun, you found and extracted your own water, generated your own fuel, made your own medicine, foretold your own weather, provided your own education. Folks, that's not a simple life.

Our life today is simple. Yeah, I know about computers, fuel-injected engines, telecommunications, the information highway, social madness in the cities, space travel, and all that. But what do you have to do with any of these things? What do you know about it? Do you fix your own car or computer? Did you design the latest space probe? Did you come up with microwavable popcorn? Let's say you did, Orville. Did you also design the heat pump that cools your house as well as warms it? Did you castrate your own cat? When was the last time you set a broken leg?

Life around you is complex, but when you flick the light switch tonight as you go to bed, chances are you don't know diddly about what just happened, and if you do, smarty-pants, chances are that that's all you know anything about.

So having a microwave oven is no more a betrayal of simple food preparation than a cast-iron pot, which you also didn't make, by the way. A microwave is just a fancier, more fragile cast-iron pot. Think of it that way.

And it's just about as useful. I don't know how we'd live without our micronuker. I bought the thing twenty years ago when I was batching, and it was a cheapie then, so it is anything but complicated. It has one switch that turns it off and on and sets the time, sort of. (The knob is so loose, you can't really count on anything, but it does still turn off and on with regularity, so . . .) All of which means I can't tell you much about how to use a microwave, but I get the impression that even the new ones are still pretty self-explanatory. Actually, I don't do any cooking in mine other than occasionally making popcorn when I don't want to go to the trouble of washing my Flecknor popcorn bucket. I use it to thaw and heat packages of ribs, soup, that sort of thing, and it does that magnificently.

When I lived in the log cabin down by the river, I didn't need a microwave, mostly because I didn't have a freezer, entirely because I didn't have electricity. And that worked fine, too. I suppose I could have looked for a kerosene-fueled freezer, and then find a wood-fired microwave oven, and . . . well, never mind.

THE SOCIETY OF FOOD

Therfore bihoveth hire a ful long spoon
That shal ete with a feend.
— CHAUCER, "THE SQUIRE'S TALE,"
The Canterbury Tales, 1387

It's a very odd thing—
As odd as can be—
That whatever Miss T. eats
Turns into Miss T.
— WALTER DE LA MARE, "MISS T."

A crust eaten in peace is better than a banquet partaken
in anxiety.
— AESOP, "THE TOWN MOUSE AND THE
COUNTRY MOUSE"

BEST FRIENDS

My favorite dining companion, simply put, is me. I wondered for years about people who are uncomfortable going
into an elegant restaurant, or humble café, and just sitting

down and eating and enjoying a meal. I don't have any trouble with that. I love to have the time to consider the food and to think about other things. Which is not to say I have trouble eating with others. I love to eat with my wife, Linda. I love her. No other way to put it. I just plain love her. And I love being with her. If there is a problem, it's that most of our meals around here are increasingly disjointed, as Antonia (now thirteen) gets older and adds her element of unpredictability to our already frantic lifestyle. Most of our meals are grabbed and eaten on the run. We eat with our evening meals balanced on our knees. Sure, it's dreadful, but that's the way it is, and I suspect we're not the only people in America for whom that is the standard.

So the simplest meal somewhere else, with or without Antonia or other friends, becomes per se an occasion. When Linda and I (w/ or w/o Antonia) go to town on errands, whether it's to our little village of Dannebrog, population 322, or Grand Island, a half hour from here, population 35,000, or to Omaha, the BIG city (600,000), a major consideration is where we are going to eat. And we *are* going to eat. We plan our travels to bang up against or straddle a mealtime. I suppose there is always the relief of not having to cook or do dishes, and we have nailed down some terrific places to eat during these adventures so there's good food, but once again, it's that wacky idea of ceremony. It's nice to sit opposite Linda and/or Antonia and eat *with* them. To look at them, talk with them. I'm not sure the food has to be good to enjoy something like that.

One of the first things I learned about Native Americans—so different from mainstream America—is that when Indian friends gather, they don't need to talk to enjoy the company. In fact, they often comment on our tendency to chatter, even when we say nothing, when there is nothing to be said. Same at a meal. I'm not sure we need to talk. There is definitely something else going on. Something, in fact, that I consider to be one of the most interesting anthropological aspects of human behavior—eating together. I consider our dogs—two of them black Labs. They are not brother and sister, but they might as well be. They are total companions. When one of them is at the vet's, the other is inconsolable, utterly confused. They can't imagine life without each other. Same with me. They adore me, just as any dogs adore their masters, even bad ones. And I'm a good one. I am the source of all good and all wrath. I'm the pack leader. Alpha male, that's me. I feed them. They don't know where food comes from. All they know is that it is there every day, twice a day. And I bring it.

So I give each dog, say, a large soup bone I get from the slaughterhouse up in town. They know where it came from. They know they each have one. So one of them eases over and sniffs the other dog's bone, because we also know nothing is ever as good as the *other* dog's bone. Teeth are bared, hackles are raised, there is growling. Okay, we have established that no matter how close the kinship between those two, when it comes to food, something else is going on. They would probably kill for each other if one was threatened, but, ah, when there's food to be considered. . . .

Enter me. I reach down to take the bone I, after all, have just given them. They can't really resist. They can't really growl. They dare not bite. But boy, are they messed up. They just don't know what to do. One thing is certain: It is not their intention to offer to share their bounty, even if it was me in the first place who put it in front of them. Food is too critical. Although they've never been faced by hunger, never mind starvation, that pain is there, deep in their hereditary memories. They've never missed a meal, and they have no intentions of voluntarily surrendering this one. They roll over on their backs, exposing their soft underbellies, saying essentially, "I may not want to share my food with you, but see? I will make myself incredibly vulnerable to you, because you are The Great and Munificent Bringer of Bones, Oh Mighty One." The bottom line is, food is food.

For them. For us, that may also hold true (and there are probably as many people hungry in this world as dogs), but there is something else, too. I know there are pack behaviors where animals—even canines—share food to maintain the social fabric of their hunting-living unit, and I suppose there was a time when we humans came to do that, too. (I would argue that there have been times in our human evolution when we actually have shown the common sense and decency of animals, but I understand that there are plenty of arguments that fly in the face of that presumption, especially when it comes to dogs. I have argued many a time that it's no coincidence that *dog* spelled backward is *god*. Nor that *kitty-cat* spelled backward is *ticky-tack,* sort of.)

But imagine what a gigantic leap it must have been when some hominid came back to the others in his blood group with a dead and half-rotted (when it comes to beef these days, we call it aged) antelope haunch he managed to pull away from some jackals, and instead of tucking it back in the corner of his cave and keeping it all for himself, fighting off anyone else who wanted some—like Lucky and Thud, my black Labs—he threw it down into the center of the group, letting everyone eat what he or she wanted. This was probably a pragmatic and not a romantic gesture, the idea being, "Me Oog give food to Bltz and Moop. Maybe tomorrow Oog take day off and Bltz and Moop find dead bear and give some to Oog?" What a cosmic leap of faith! Lucky is a doggy genius, but I don't think he's figured out that notion—not to mention that it wouldn't work. It doesn't matter how generous Lucky might be, Thud isn't going to share his supper, ever, with anyone.

How many times were Oog, Oog Jr., Oog III, and Oog XXII disappointed before the arrangement finally fell into place? Who knows?

Thing is, one could argue that we still do it to some extent, but I think we've gone way beyond that. I suppose one could surmise that I buy a beer for my brother-in-law Steve Lingendinger because he'll probably buy one for me down the line, and there are some boneheads who keep track of such transactions, making sure no one falls behind or that they don't get ahead. But there are others, like me, who treasure the system where no one keeps track, simply because that's the way the world should work, and maybe the way Heaven does—no one keeping track.

OF COURSE I'LL RESPECT YOU AT DESSERT

One could argue that some men still operate on the keeping-track system when it comes to dating: "Gork buy Heidi supper, Heidi make kissy-face, or even wiggle-wiggle." There are women, some named Heidi, who probably also think that way. That puts a remarkably low price on a fairly important commodity. Guys who think like this wind up with women like Heidi, another case like beans and opera, if I may say so. And before long, Heidi's not even getting a free meal.

I submit nonetheless that the same transaction could be made, maybe to everyone's greater satisfaction, by simply giving the young lady fifty dollars. (I understand this is also a tradition that has some currency, but this is a book about food.) I therefore also submit that eating with a woman—or *feeding* a woman, when that is the case, as it so often is even in this new, gender-enlightened America—is a good deal more than an exchange of valuables, just as dating is about more than sex.

I want you to imagine this scenario, scarcely an unlikely one. You spot this ravishing woman you would really like to get to know. Yes, there is a wholesome lust there, but more than that, as you talk with her, you enjoy her wit, her way, her laugh, her honesty, her wonderful common sense (which is to say, she agrees with you about almost everything), and while you would probably ask her out with little more motivation than being able to rub up against her while going through the door into the movies, you have the feeling too that there may be something more to this one. There could be a . . . er . . . uh . . . future here, if you catch my drift. This may be the one.

So you ask her out, and what do you ask her to do with you? Certainly not go out to eat! That would be the single most stupid thing you could possibly do!! Do you really want this woman to see you performing a basic biological function? Would you invite her to watch you blow your nose? Light a fart? Pee against a truck tire? (Okay, considering the kind of women you date, maybe you would, but there are some of the rest of us who find our dates somewhere other than bikers' bars.) And yet you invite her to come and watch you eat.

Have you forgotten the hundreds of times you dribbled soup down your front? The tons of salad dressing still chemically bonded with your mustache? The quarts of root beer blown out your nose? The bales of spinach that have stuck to your teeth? The times you drank the water from the finger bowl, used a butter knife to cut your steak, or ordered the restaurant manager as an entrée from a French menu? What happens if you choke on a crouton or drop a garlic-buttered snail into your crotch? You know how a Wendy's fish sandwich squirts tartar sauce all over the dashboard of your car when you order one; you know what's going to happen when you sit down

and try to eat . . . well, *anything* with this woman you're trying to impress. Why would you put yourself in a situation like this? Why would you do something so patently stupid? You're going to be so nervous that you're not going to be able to eat anyway, and even if you do, your ticklish bowel is going to kick into action. If you're lucky, your stomach will only growl through the entire movie (better choose an action film with lots of explosions and gunfights to cover up the gastric fireworks, you think to yourself). If you're not lucky . . . well, better sit toward the back of the theater so you can get to the men's room in a hurry.

Why, why, why, why, why, why, why?!! You'll ask yourself that a thousand times during your supper date anyway, so let's take a look at it now. Trust me. I'm an anthropologist. I know about such things. Don't be afraid. Once again, it's a matter of vulnerability. You take her out to eat not in spite of all the reasons above but *because* of them. You are Gork, and you are one fearsome silverback. The clan wouldn't trust you if you were a patsy. They are drawn to you because you are a fearsome, testosterone-drenched male. Your size and ferocity spell survival for others—especially potential mates—and that's with a capital *S*. So, how then do you convince this tender, soft creature you want to, uh, talk philosophy with that you're fearsome, sure, but you have your tender side, too? Like Lucky and Thud, you growl when you need to, shake the ground with your barks when the situation calls for it, face down intruders, protect your family, play the tough game . . . and then, when you encounter someone you need to show deference to, The Grand Master, for example, you roll over and show your soft belly, you crouch low, you whine and pule. If you need to, you pee uncontrollably. What else can you do to show your willingness to demonstrate your weaknesses, your vulnerability to this person you want to approach? How can you demonstrate your willingness to share the unshareable and convince her to do the same?

Well, in our case—in a man's case—he is never more vulnerable than when he's eating. No woman likes the way any man eats, so what you do is let her watch you eat, in all your manly slobbishness. Jeez, your primal psyche says, if she doesn't collapse in laughter, point at me, humiliate me, walk out on me, throw things at me when I use the wrong fork, dribble gravy on my tie, eat the table bouquet, spill my wine, lick my knife, order an artichoke rare, save the shells off the snails for my seashell collection ... MAYBE SHE WON'T LAUGH THREE WEEKS FROM NOW WHEN I TAKE OFF MY CLOTHES AND SHE SEES ME AT MY FUNNIEST!

Okay, you're saying, this is still a matter of, you should excuse the expression, tit for tat. Guys put themselves through this because they want something. That's not a very profound social process—this for that. Okay, then what's going on when we choose to eat with other people even in situations where we don't want sex or a mate? Why do we put ourselves in a situation for potential humiliation at times like that?

And we do. One of the ways I make my living is as a banquet speaker. Nebraska is not a big convention state, but I don't believe there's an organization from Pork Breeders to Nebraska Bankers that doesn't have its annual convention ... complete with the annual banquet. There was a time when I attended annual meetings—and banquets—not as a guest

and a speaker, but as a participant. I sat down with colleagues, admired masters, and adoring followers, to
eat. And here's where the quid pro quo thing really
falls apart. Here are people from whom you want little
more than respect, maybe recognition, perhaps only

notice. So, why in the world would you therefore put yourself
in a situation so utterly fraught with the potential for embarrassing mistakes as a banquet? This isn't even just a matter of
you and a woman eating in the privacy of a McDonald's
booth or even at a table in a fancy Chinese place. Here you
are, surrounded by people you really need, whose respect
you desperately want—there's always another woman, but
another career?!—and here you are, eating. What an incredibly stupid strategy!

Unless you are essentially saying, "See? I'm no threat. I
trust you. No matter how much of a doofus I am tonight, no
matter what a mess I make, even if I only put myself in this
situation of a potential mess, I believe in you enough that I
am willingly accepting this jeopardy. I'll even sit here and lis-
ten to a boring speaker for an hour after we eat to show I'm
not reluctant about putting myself in a situation where my
stomach might embarrass me. That's how much I trust you.
And I can see you trust me. I guess we must be buddies then,
huh?"

HOW THE SAVAGES DO IT

When I first started going to Omaha Indian gatherings, I saw
all these disgracefully mistreated poor people around me.
And I grew very fond of them. They inevitably had their
feast, a collection of food that sometimes bordered on the
pathetic. I was already fat, well fed, and even rich, in comparison with the poverty around me in these gatherings. It
seemed to me utterly inappropriate that I eat the food of

these people. So, when time came around for the requisite feast, I excused myself and left. I thought I was doing the socially responsible thing.

Wrong-o. What the Omahas need is not a couple extra bites of food but respect, friends, and allies. What kind of ally won't eat with you? they must have thought. In fact, the real union between me and the Omahas, now *my* people, came when I breached a powerful social rule and actually asked for food, something you don't do among the Omahas. As I sat at countless handgames, a kind of social activity that involves dance, music, food, and all sorts of cultural reinforcements, I came to look forward to the feast that followed. I like Indian soup, yes, but I really came to like—love—my company. But one thing bothered me: early on, when the Omahas saw me as a guest rather than a brother, they treated me as a guest. I was fed first in the feast, and I got certain extra consideration in the handing out of the foods. For example, I was served a slice or two of white, American style bread from plastic wrappers, while others, certainly all the Indians, were handed brown, fist-size hunks of a dark, fragrant bread served from bushel baskets. I later learned this is frybread, a Native American standard food. Since frybread is regular food and pasty white bread is an expensive treat, they were honoring me by offering me the best they had to offer.

Frybread

To begin with, I don't think you can make really good Indian frybread unless you're an Indian. On the other hand, just as you can judge and treasure a white girl by her mashed potatoes, if you are courting an Indian girl, her frybread should be your pride and joy.

Frybread came to the Indians from their enemy, American soldiers. Soldiers couldn't really haul around baking ovens and yeast cultures, so they learned to raise bread with baking powder and fry it in lard. Indians, not being invited into a lot of white folks' kitchens but having their share of contact with the military, learned how to make frybread rather than croissants. Since lard and unbleached flour have been fairly consistent government-surplus commodity foods distributed on reservations, frybread is one historic food that has survived even while it has faded away within white culture, including army mess halls.

Mix a couple cups of unbleached flour, a little salt, some milk, a tablespoon of baking powder, and a little lard or solid shortening thoroughly. Drop round, flattened wads of this mixture, about the size of the top half—okay, or the bottom half—of a hamburger bun, into hot lard or cooking oil hot enough to make the bread bubble and growl vigorously. (You can test the heat with smaller wads.) When the breads are warm brown on one side, turn them until the other side is just as golden. Pull from the fat and drain on newspaper. And that's it. If it isn't delicious, you've done it wrong.

Sometimes Indians put cooked hamburger in the middle of the bread before deep-fat frying it and call it an Indian hamburger. Or they make extra large frybreads—plate-size—and then shovel standard taco fixings on top of them—ground beef, refried beans, lettuce, cheese, salsa, tomato, peppers—and call the result Indian tacos. They're good, too, but I'm a purist and prefer the traditional breads as is. Or as are.

When I asked Linda for her advice on this recipe,

she gave me the best possible answer: "Buy the mix." Commercial frybread mix is not easy to find, but some western markets now carry mixes that have been formulated and marketed from Indian reservations, which means they have to be good. I used to buy a hundred or two frybreads when I went to the Omaha Tribal Powwow every August, package them two or three to a package, and freeze them, but it was not a satisfying process. The breads get soggy and when I warmed them in the micro-nuker, they got tough—not the sort of violence frybread deserves.

Look for the mixes, or write directly to the manufacturer. Our favorite right now is The Woodenknife Company, PO Box 104, Interior, SD 57750.

Hamburgers

Hamburgers should be cooked outdoors on the grill, right? They're pretty good when cooked in a deep, heavy sauce of soup mix—onion soup, cream of mushroom, tomato soup—but they are clearly best on the grill. Make yourself up *big* burgers, not those wimpy little quarter-pounders. (Where did anyone ever get the notion that a quarter of a pound, four measly ounces, is a generous helping of ground beef anyway?! Any decent cook would be embarrassed to brag about a quarter-pound serving of meat.) On a grill, volume is especially important since, even more than is the case with steaks, thickness and size affects juiciness. Mix some chopped onion in with the meat, and add a little barbecue, Worcestershire, or soy sauce. That's the trick.

Just as with steaks, turn the burgers only once—first when the juice comes up through the meat, and second when the juice comes up through the meat again. That's medium rare. And extra good.

Well, the more I watched that bread handed out, and the more I smelled it, the more I lusted for it. I finally did the unthinkable and asked my hosts if I could possibly forgo the Wonder Bread crap and maybe have a piece of that dark brown bread in the bushel baskets. They gave me one, perhaps a little embarrassed at the time that they were cornered into giving plain old Indian frybread to this guest, but then they laughed at my obvious approval, my enthusiasm, and from then on, they made a point of making sure I got frybread, even if there wasn't enough to go around. They came to like the idea of a white guy preferring frybread to the fancy stuff that comes in plastic bags. They joked that I was about to become an Omaha by ingestion, and when I was adopted into the tribe in 1967, there was some joking that I would almost surely be given the name I had earned—Frybread! I'm not sure that's just a joke. Sometimes we really do become what we eat. By eating Omaha food with the Omahas, I became an Omaha. Perhaps it was only a matter of the reverse: it was clear when I was not eating Omaha food with the Omahas that I was scarcely an Omaha. Maybe I really only lusted for Omaha food once the mystic transformation had begun.

One of my favorite food anecdotes, one of those enlightening moments when truth is revealed, came to me when I was standing around with a bunch of older Indian men—all of them now lamentably gone. We were waiting for a social occasion of some sort to begin, and so we were talking and enjoying a warm autumn sun. A couple little kids ran by, and one of them, wearing khaki shorts, was a mess: obviously, he had stuffed a chocolate bar in his pocket, it had melted, and the entire right side of his pants were stained by the chocolate and the oil from it. Clyde Sheridan laughed and said, "It reminds me of when we were at the Genoa Indian School." The other elders laughed, too, and nodded their agreement.

I didn't understand the reference. Since it is impolite in Omaha society to ask questions, I said something like, "The Genoa Indian School had something to do with stained pants . . ." The Omahas are always sensitive to the confusion of the white man, and so they explained to me that while they were students at the Genoa, Nebraska, boarding school for Indians, they were fed white man's food. Don't get me started about the savagery inflicted on Plains Indians by white invaders. The cruelty is unthinkable, and of course the irony is the notion that *we* were bringing civilization to *them*. What a load of crapola!

Anyway, these distinguished elders told me that the white administrators at the school did everything they could to erase the beautiful native cultures of their wards, including feeding them only the white man's wretched food. So the children, separated for months, even years from their families, devised a clever scheme to thwart those efforts. Someone brought from home a small cast-iron pan, which the children hid in the woods along the Loup River, not far from the school. They filched small scraps of fat from pork and beef served in the school's dining hall and stashed them *in their pockets*. There was scarcely a pair of pants in the entire school, my Omaha mentors told me, that didn't bear that distinctive stain pattern! The children would sneak from the school when they could, pick up an ear of corn from the surrounding fields—not a difficult task at all—take it to the woods where they had hidden their pan, build a small fire, and with the filched fat, parch their corn. And eat Indian food. And all the efforts of the white man to destroy their Indianness were washed away by the cleansing purge of the Indian fare.

SOUL FOOD

Is that nonsense? Do you think that's nonsense? I sure don't. I think it is an honesty and reality we all believe in, whether we admit it or not. Those are precisely the reasons every family, every culture, has foods it considers not a source of physical nourishment—lutefisk, collard greens, *runzas,* dumplings, and duck—but a source of cultural and spiritual renewal. Soul food, if you like—the perfect phrase for what it is.

Frankly, I think hamburger is the soul food for Americans. Mick's duck is soul food for him and his comrades. Salmon patties, creamed peas, and macaroni and cheese are soul food for my Linda. Some folks are embarrassed by that because they think they shouldn't acknowledge stupid things like soul, culture, spirit, renewal, history, and depth. Well, screw 'em. Real men understand such things.

Lovely Linda's Salmon Patties

I asked Linda for a copy of her recipe for salmon patties, much to her amazement. She knows how I feel about them. There has never been a doubt in my mind but that feeding me Catholic food on Fridays is her way to win me and my soul over to the Pope. Be careful with this stuff, Orangemen. You'll find yourself twitching to cross yourself next Sunday morning and dropping to your knees every time you read a Latinism in a footnote, if you're not careful.

I note with some amusement that Linda omits any comment about the civilizing influences I use on this traditional Friday Nebraska Czech Catholic fare: Coleman's mustard on the macaroni and cheese, Tabasco sauce on the patties. "Crimes against the Cross," she calls it. By the way, the phrase *haute cuisine* is Czech for "Death to the Infidel."

Linda says, "I can't believe you want this recipe. We ate it on Friday nights as a side dish with macaroni and cheese, right out of the box. Real haute cuisine. I still make it sometimes when I'm feeling nostalgic [Author's note: Every Friday night].

2 tall cans pink salmon
2 eggs
handful of saltine crackers

"Drain the salmon and remove the skin and bones. Flake the salmon.

"Mix in the eggs and crush enough saltine crackers into it to hold together. Form into patties and lightly fry in a tablespoon or two of oil until browned on both sides.

"Patties *must* be eaten with lots of ketchup or the ambience is lost."

Poor child. Little does she know.

Food is more important than you can imagine. You can go a long time without eating. You can scratch and scrounge and piece together what you need to survive. But that's not what I'm talking about. What you need even more is that stuff that lets you maintain yourself as what you are, not just stay alive.

Cultures survive on rice, but rice is not, strictly speaking, the stuff of central Plains cuisine. In my family, rice meant one thing, and I grew up thinking *that* was rice. I don't know how Mom cooked it. This evening I'm going to ask Linda to find out. As I recall, she cooked white rice with milk in a double boiler. (I can *see* that red-and-white enameled double boiler at this very moment, steaming on a gas stove!) And she cooked it and cooked it and cooked it and cooked it. All day long.

By evening, she had a pot of white, pasty starch, for all the world like the library paste I ate during the day in school. Well, hell, it smelled so good. How could I resist it?! Anyway, this homogeneous white paste was plopped onto our supper plates and then we poured burned butter over it. And that was supper. This was not a poverty dish. Not, at least, as far as I was concerned. It was a special treat. God, I loved that stuff. There was nothing else with that meal—no bread, meat, salad, dessert, nothing. That gorgeous glop needed nothing else to be perfect. Just rice paste and burnt butter.

Now, imagine for a moment my confusion the first time I saw an advertisement on television for Uncle Ben's *fluffy* rice. And forget that in my family, in my mother's delicate vocabulary, a fluff is a fart. I knew they didn't mean that. Well, at least I suspected they didn't mean that. But I considered, intellectually, my mother's rice paste and I could not, straining every fiber of my generous imagination, apply the word *fluffy* to it. God, a tablespoon of that stuff weighed twelve pounds! And then you add burnt butter!

Now I know the difference. I eat in fancy Chinese restaurants, because I'm a fancy guy. I know how the rest of the world sees rice, as a bunch of separate little grains. So, at this very moment, which do you think I would most like to have? (A) Fluffy rice or (B) Mom's rice paste?

Mom's Rice Paste

Mom doesn't waste a lot of time. And she knows, from having a son who has been a folklorist-researcher for thirty-five years, what most people's expectations are when it comes to things like recipes. She knows most people think of recipes as precise formulas; she also knows that most recipes aren't. So brace yourself. She's not going to waste a lot of your time with explanations or apologies here.

"I don't measure any of the ingredients. I put about one cup of rice in a saucepan, add about one cup of water or enough to cover the rice. Simmer until the water is boiled down. Stir often. Then put the rice in the top of a double boiler. Cover with milk and about 3/4 cup sugar. Add more milk when needed. Stir often. Cook slowly until thick.

"Brown about one cube of *butter* in a small frying pan. Serve over rice.

"Use regular rice, not the quick or one-minute rice."

There is some considerable difficulty in sharing someone else's soul food, comfort food, home food, Mom's food. When the outsider goes into these situations, he or she doesn't carry along all the emotional load that adds flavor, color, depth, and substance to what is otherwise just *food*. What's important is that you consider not the food but the context. And, as a man, I sincerely believe you are in a better situation to do that than a woman is. You may like the food; I like lutefisk, even though the people who think of it only as a soul food often also think of it as dreadful. My wife's family loves *kolaches*, a Czech pastry that doesn't strike me as much more than bread with jam on it, but not as good. What's important is not that I like it but that I understand why she likes it. Fellas, if you intend to survive, yet prosper, with women, or woman, you damn well better get that straight. What's important is not that

you like it but that they are sharing it with you. Remember the dogs? Don't growl and try to show how sophisticated you are. Eat it and gush about how great it is. If she won't meet you later out behind the washhouse, her mother will. Vulnerability has its rewards: as far as I'm concerned, the only completely laudable thing George Bush did during his mercifully brief presidency, maybe during his painfully long tenure at the public trough for that matter, was puke on the Japanese prime minister. I felt sorry for him but appreciated the poetic, metaphoric Pearl Harbor.

On the other hand—and even women understand this (it may be a part of Woman School, but how the hell would we know?)—the most important thing you can do in courtship is to share your soul food with her. Doesn't matter if she doesn't like it. Tell her all the stories about it, your memories, your connection with it, the power that it has in your life's experience. Tell her that it may not be very good as food, but it is important to you: "This white rice paste has meaning." You've shared your vulnerability. You rolled over and showed her your soft underbelly even though you may not have been all that enthusiastic about sharing your food. You showed her you trusted her not to insult those things closest to your soul.

You say she went ahead and insulted it anyway? Well, doofus, think about it. There may be a lesson there. If she can't figure this out and appreciate it, what do you think is in store for you in the future? If she says something like, "I'm not crazy about this, Buford, but it's so sweet of you to share it with me," well, think about that, too. Then hope she shares her private, family, cultural soul food with you, and use what you've learned here in Man School to handle the situation well.

And yes, you're welcome for the great advice.

JUST KIDDING

There is one meal companion no man wants, ever—a child. One of the biggest joys of the annual Christmas and Thanksgiving feasts is that there is often a children's table, off in another room, like the kitchen, sometimes with an intervening door. Good riddance. Nor is it simply a matter that children are messy. Men are messy. The problem is that children are children, and that is not easily remedied. I know a couple who raised their son within a dining system where they ate at the dining-room table and he ate in the kitchen. Women think this is dreadful. Men dream of it. This is why men have for millennia so often disappeared with war and hunting parties—so they wouldn't have to eat with children. It doesn't have anything to do with testosterone, as psychologists—usually women with too much testosterone of their own—would have us believe. The men are simply tired of eating with children, and two places where women will not let children go are fighting and killing.

That last paragraph will get me into trouble enough, I'm sure, so I won't venture into the minefield of cultures where men and women eat separately. Eating being the erotic experience it is, or can be, I wouldn't even recommend it. I was, however, once invited by a friend in Germany to go to a neighboring farmer's birthday party. A birthday party for a grown man? Didn't sound like the sort of thing I would enjoy. My friend advised, however, that as an anthropologist, not to mention a pig, I might enjoy the experience. So I went. And boy, was I glad I did.

We entered a room dominated by a big table where there were already six or eight very Germanic men. As we came through the door, they greeted us loudly, and shouted "Prosit!" (*Prosit* is a German drinking toast.) They poured themselves some more

schnapps and beer and toasted us again. Turns out, that's what they do at a German birthday party whenever a new guest comes in, and there were maybe twenty guests in on this particular event. After everyone was there, we pretty much toasted things in general. Then when men started to leave, late in the afternoon, we toasted their departure.

There were no women at the party. Well, that's not quite true. All the wives were there, but they were in another part of the house. While we talked tractors, beer, politics, and weather (everyone was very struck by the fact that the day before there had been quite a clap of thunder, giving me get the impression that north German weather isn't quite like central American Plains weather!), the women were talking about . . . well, I don't know what they were talking about. Every hour or so the wife of the birthday boy brought in another tray or dish of food for us, shook her head, clucked her tongue at our cigars, raised both hands and threw them forward and retreated, or advanced, back to her lady friends. I can imagine those who would see this as a degrading exercise in sexism. I don't know why. It seemed pretty obvious to me that the ladies were having a lot of fun, probably a lot more than they would have had in our room, and were generally grateful that they were spared the noise, smell, and company at our end of the house. Our mood, if anything, was a sense of gratitude that the ladies understood our maleness. If there were superior and inferior stations, I didn't spot any evidence.

The toughest situation, to get back to where I started this

digression, is when a man-food kind of man is in the situation I touched on before, when my dad had to feed Cousin Wayne and me. How does a man cook for children? I think he should cook like a man. It won't kill them to eat man food for a while. They'll learn something from the experience. Let them eat what you eat. The last thing you want to do is try to fix them what they're used to. Make this an adventure. Take them to the place where you can eat with sticks. Take them to the place where no one speaks English, let them eat menudo, and then tell them what it is. Let 'em eat ribs with their fingers and then hose them off in the driveway, sort of like you do when you're eating alone. Show them how to make Indian jerky and frybread. Make them something they've never eaten before so they can't compare it with anything. Tell 'em that's the way it's supposed to taste. Tell 'em it's Rooshen Fried Cabbage.

Dad's Daffy Doughnuts
Corn Fritters

You don't have to tell me that these two foods I am recommending as children food are not exactly nutritional masterpieces. What I used them for was to get me through the damned day, fill the little boogers' bellies, and provide them with some entertainment short of burning down the garage or torturing the cat, two of the things kids would rather do than eat. As I have repeated probably to your distraction, food is a lot more than nutrition. Think of this as an exercise in teaching and learning. Either the children in your charge will despise these foods and plead with their mother or other parents never again to throw them into the lions' pit of child care you call home, or they will find them wonderfully disreputable and beg for them the next time they are in your care. Either way, you win.

Obviously, a big part of Dad's Daffy Doughnuts is the name. My children still speak of them with awe. I heated up a pot of cooking oil and broke out a tube of store-bought biscuit mix. The children were forbidden to enter the kitchen because I didn't want them around the hot oil, but also because I didn't want them around me, so I cloaked the process in the mystery of surprise. I formed the biscuit dough into wacky, silly, crazy, stupid, even naughty ("dog poop") forms before dropping them into the hot oil. When they were golden brown, or crispy auburn, or occasionally burntish brown, I dipped them out with a perforated ladle, drained them on newspaper, and let them cool a little. Then the kids got to come in, *but weren't allowed to look at the doughnuts.* I put the doughnuts and a half cup of sugar in a brown paper bag and let the kids shake the bag vigorously (kids like anything vigorous) until the doughnuts were completely frosted with sugar.

Then we took them out and put them on our plates, which for this occasion were more sheets of newspaper. And they guessed what I had in mind when I formed my biscuit-dough sculptures. Then we ate them. The color and shape and company almost always led to scatological guesses, especially once children knew they could get away with that kind of language around me. But I consider that part of the learning process, too. Cowboys called such doughnuts bear sign, a polite term for bear shit, so the children were operating within honored, historic linguistic parameters. Explain that to your kids. They'll be grateful.

DDDs are megaton gut bombs, believe me, and the children won't be hungry again for days. Sometimes I heightened the mystery by concealing things inside the dough—bits of wienie, gumdrops, pickle slices, tomato chunks, anything I could find in the fridge or cupboard. Then they had to guess what they'd just eaten. And I told them it was dinosaur meat, snot, cat poop, whatever I could find in my demented mind. They loved it. Then I made them promise not to tell their mother what we ate and what we called it, and we had a secret they could keep from an adult, the only thing a kid likes better than arson, mayhem, or eating.

All of which goes double for corn fritters, another deep-fat-fried gut bomb that looks like something vaguely excremental, can be used to contain mysterious surprise foods, and lies in the belly like gravel pudding. When my offspring were children, they loved me to cook up a mess of corn fritters, because we would feed the leftovers to our dog and laugh hilariously all evening as she farted with such vigor she offended even herself. She'd fart, jump up, and look disgustedly back at where the noise and odor had emanated, as if the fart had materialized from thin air, somewhere in the vicinity of the far end of her tail, with no actual connection to herself. Maybe she was just being coy. Anyway, we thought it was pretty funny, a confession that will probably get me in trouble with the animal rights people.

I mix a cup of flour, a teaspoon or so of baking powder, and a little salt with three or four well-beaten eggs. Then I added a can of whole kernel corn. *The Joy of Cooking*, a book I trust and cherish, recommends mashing the corn all up and draining it before adding it to the batter, but I prefer to drain the whole corn and add it as is to the batter. Not to mention that my technique involves a lot less work. Heat a pot of cooking oil. Test it with

smallish fritters until it seethes and pops when you drop them in. Then drop tablespoon-size dollops into the fat, turning them with a fork, until they are brown on both sides, which they will do pretty quickly. As with Dad's Daffy Doughnuts, I often inserted bits of bologna, Spam, pineapple, banana, apple—whatever I could find— inside the dollops to give us something to discuss while we sat on the kitchen floor eating the fritters.

I love maple syrup—the more real, the better—but once, when I was dumping fritters into the kids, I found out, too late, that we were out of maple syrup. So I heated up a saucepan of water, added sugar until the liquid was thick as syrup, and flavored it with vanilla to taste. It was absolutely delicious. At the time, I just told the children it was Dad's Secret Recipe Syrup. Then I put the leftover syrup in a mason jar, let it cool, and put it in the refrigerator for next time, it was so good. As the liquid cooled and reached a saturation point with the sugar, crystals began to form in the jar; and the next time we needed syrup, we found that we had a crystal bowl, like a geode, with a center full of syrup nectar. I showed the phenomenon to the kids and announced that I had been lying all along: the syrup was actually rock juice. And that's what it was from then on: rock juice. You could flavor your syrup with cinnamon, peppermint, just about anything, I suppose. And you can call it anything you want, too.

Another secret to feeding children is to avoid the

potential of a messy table by suggesting you "picnic" directly on the kitchen floor. They'll think it's great fun, and then you just mop up the mess or wad up the newspapers you spread beforehand and throw them in the fireplace. Use paper plates, eat the fritters, syrup and all, with your fingers, throw everyone in the bathtub immediately after eating, which you were probably instructed to do anyway, and you're taking care of two problems at once—cleaning the kids and cleaning the dishware. The kids will think you're a genius, and so will the Little Lady if she doesn't find out exactly what went on, a contingency you have taken care of by swearing the children to pirates' oaths of secrecy before supper.

A TIME AND A PLACE

A man hath no better thing under the sun, than to eat,
and to drink, and to be merry.
>
> —ECCLESIASTES 8:15

You must sit down, says Love, and taste my meat:
So I did sit and eat . . .
>
> —GEORGE HERBERT,
> *The Temple*, 1633

Good bread, good meat
Good God, let's eat.
>
> —ANONYMOUS GRACE

Only in the Midwest is overeating still considered an act of
heroism.
>
> —JACK NICHOLSON. I DON'T KNOW
> WHEN OR WHERE HE SAID THIS, AND
> PROBABLY NEITHER DOES HE, BUT JIM
> HARRISON SAYS HE SAID IT AND
> THAT'S GOOD ENOUGH FOR ME.

CARPE DIET

I suppose there are two good times to eat: (1) when you have planned a meal and (2) when you haven't. There is the elegance and confidence, the considered pleasure of a well-planned meal, but there is a good deal to be said for the spontaneity of food suddenly there, eaten by impulse and inspiration. I suppose my example, to follow, isn't really a *food* issue but another of those cases where there is a good deal more than taste and nutrition to ingestion. Once I was a vigorous wine maker. I even ran a small shop selling supplies for amateur wine makers. I even got to the point where I brokered wine grapes, bringing in truckloads of wine grapes from California and selling them to others in case lots.

The problem always was that when the grapes came in, there they were. I had no refrigeration or storage facilities, so everyone knew that when they ordered grapes from me, I would call the day they arrived, and it was up to them to pick them up *immediately*. I did what I could to help my friends and customers by making some of my equipment available to them—for example, I had a hand-turned grape crusher that made the task of stemming and crushing tons of grapes much easier. So, anywhere between six and a dozen wine makers would gather at my place when the grapes came in and set to work, taking the fruit from the grapes and crushing them. The work usually went well into the night, which was inconvenient perhaps but served its purpose: I once got a call from a buyer who said she had found a spider in the middle of a tightly compacted bunch of Zinfandel grapes and wondered what she could do, since there might be other small creatures in others of her two hundred pounds of grapes. I explained that the best thing to do in such circumstances is to stem the grapes at night, when you can't see what's going into the wine vat. Grapes picked in large vineyards, whether picked by machine or man, include not only bugs, but occasional snakes, bird nests, and who knows what else. Doesn't matter. The processes of fermentation eat it all up, cleanse it, disarm it, turn it into wine. Simply doesn't matter.

So, there we were on this cool autumn evening, a dozen of us young men and women, joyously stemming our grapes, laughing, joking, working, drinking a little of last year's vintage. It's a voluptuous process, anyway; for example, I showed them a little trick from France, where workers in the vineyards avail themselves of a special treat in the form of *paradis,* the name being self-explanatory. At the moment a grape bursts and spills its juices, it also releases minute quantities of incredibly delicious, sense-provoking, highly volatile perfumes—so wonderful they are indeed labeled "paradise." You put your nose right down into the crusher or the vat beneath it. Someone turns the handle, and wham! there you are, in Paradise.

We stemmed, sniffed, and worked late into the night, pulling grapes from their stems—a messy business, but it has to be done. Then one of the young women paused, looked at her fingers that had been drenched in the sweet grape juice now for hours, sticky, sugary—and she tasted. "Wow," she said. She sucked her finger in delight. "Hey, everyone," she said, "Lick your fingers!"

Another young woman in the group then took the notion to a higher level: "I have a better idea. Let's lick each other's fingers!"

This is an interesting study, I think, in ethnogastronomy. The juice was good, at any rate. Licking a young woman's fingers seems a good idea. Having a young woman lick your fingers poses interesting potential. Now, put them all together, and you have . . . culinary opportunism, and I recommend it.

I don't know how many times I have been in the wild and discovered a foodways opportunity. Once, stranded along the highway just south of Nebraska City with a flat tire and no workable car jack, I noticed that the plum bushes along the ditch were heavy with purple fruit. We ate all we could while we waited for the tire to be fixed and filled everything we had with those plums so we could enjoy more when we got home. It is probably sinful (like licking someone else's grapey fingers) because it is so great (like someone licking your grapey fingers) but I take enormous pleasure in eating wild asparagus immediately upon picking it, dripping with juice, fresh and crisp. Is it sanitary? Oh, come on!

Wild Fruit Wines

Wine making is an ancient and simple process, but making good wines is a little more complicated. Don't get started unless you want to do it right, and then read up in your local library on how to make good wines from start to finish. I know there are a lot of folks out there making drinkable substances, usually heavy with sugar and yeast, but I'm talking good wine here. If nothing else, use Dad's old recipe, but for heaven's sake, use a good wine yeast, not bread yeast. Pioneers used to make mock apple pies out of soda crackers, but while they may have been passable, they weren't apple pies. You can make wine with bread yeast, but it's going to be closer to bread than wine. If you don't have a wine and beer maker's shop in your area, check the advertisements in an *Old Farmers' Almanac*; there are always ads there for wine-making supplies.

SAUCE FOR THE GOOSE

On the other hand, I think of my buddy Dan the Plumber, who was out making his regional rounds one spring weekend. He's an outdoorsman. He just drives around looking things over, not necessarily looking for a new fishing hole or place suitable for a deer stand. He just drives around and soaks up nature. Anyway, he happened to drive by one of his favorite wild asparagus hunting spots and while he was there, he decided he'd walk around the ditches and woods a while and see what was going on. Well, what was going on was the peak of wild asparagus season. And, it appeared, it was a good year. Everywhere he looked he saw fat, tender, young spears stabbing up from the warm, moist soil. And he started picking. He filled two large coolers he happened to have in his pickup truck with the wonderful stuff. He filled the backseat. He filled the passenger side of the front seat. Maybe two hundred pounds of asparagus. And he saw visions of home-canned asparagus on his family's cellar shelves for the entire span of the coming year.

That's the part of this story that explores food and how a man looks at it. The next scene is not quite so pretty. Dan thought he saw yet another opportunity here, one that would warm the cockles of his bride's heart. It was, after all, Mother's Day. So he went busting home as fast as he could, hauled all that raw asparagus into his wife's kitchen, and when she came home from church with the kids, beaming with the warmth of his own generosity, ol' Dan wished her a very happy Mother's Day and even offered to haul the pressure cooker and boxes of canning jars up from the basement so she could get started putting up that, oh, maybe two hundred quarts of asparagus while the stuff was still cool and fresh.

As it turned out, this was not precisely what she had in mind for Mother's Day. She was not only not grateful, she was downright insulted. In fact, she told him to leave her kitchen and take all that asparagus with him and she briefly but clearly explained that she meant right now. That's how we heard the story, when Dan came to our house with a generous gift of twenty or thirty pounds of asparagus about noon. As I recall, my wife took a handful, about enough for supper, and then repeated a lot of what she and Kim had apparently both learned when they went to Woman School, since not only the text but also the rhythm were remarkably similar. I heard later that Dan went to a couple other places bearing his Mother's Day gifts before he finally just gave up and threw his prize asparagus into a ditch somewhere. This culinary opportunism, it turned out, was not well considered.

When I was deep into my wine making, I had the remarkable good fortune to have an uncle working in the warehouse of the largest local produce wholesaler. On Fridays now and then, especially before long weekends, he'd call me up and say, "Rog, we have two cases of Catawba grapes and maybe a hundred and twenty pounds of Thompson seedless grapes that are on the edge. A little moldy but not bad. We gotta get rid of them, and if you want 'em, you can have 'em all for five bucks." I picked up the grapes, discarded the worst of them (although as with bugs, a little mold isn't that much of a problem), and made a little wine. Well, one time he called and said, "You're not going to believe this, and I won't even go into the story why, but we have five hundred pounds of strawberries in pretty good shape but what with the holidays coming up, we gotta get rid of them. You want 'em?"

Hmmm. Strawberries. You can make wine out of just about anything, but actually, I'm not all that fond of strawberries anyway, so . . . "How much do you want for them?"

"Twenty bucks."

Wow, twenty bucks for a quarter ton of fruit. It might be fun. What the heck. "Sure, I'll be right over."

I hauled the strawberries home and filled my press with maybe fifty pounds. I turned the screw tight. Maybe a table-spoon of juice came out. I turned the screw a little tighter. Another teaspoon. Oh boy. Now what? I didn't have much time at the moment to fool with the problem, so I just crushed the whole mess, added the chemicals that keep wines from turning bad, and threw it all into my largest vat with a gen-erous dose of some good wine yeast.

During the following week I punched down the cap on that mess a couple times a day, and it seemed to be going well. It smelled terrific, and as the fermentation pro-gressed, the juices seemed to be separating from the fruit's solids. As it turned out, the processes of fermentation sep-arated the juice from the pulp and pressing was not neces-sary at all. The nectar just ran out of the pulp. When the fermentation stopped, I started to siphon the liquid off, in the process getting just a little of the yeasty, raw wine in my mouth. Wow. Was it ever good! I mean, *really* good. I wound up with about sixty gallons of raw wine, which I let settle and clear, and then put in a good oak barrel for fur-ther aging.

A month later I pulled the top bung from the barrel to top it off. Wine evaporates through the wood of a barrel, and in many ways that's good. It enhances the flavor and alcohol content, for example. But wine (except sherry) doesn't like air, so you have to keep topping that barrel off so the wine has as little exposure to air as possible. I knocked the big wooden plug out of the hole on the top of the barrel and WHAM! I was hit by a perfume that was for all the world like the *paradis* of freshly crushed grapes. Incredible. I sampled the wine while I had the barrel open. It was pure nectar, the most voluptuous, erotic wine I had tasted in my life. The color was a luminescent pink. Gorgeous.

The next time I had guests I thought would appreciate the experience, I knocked the plug out again, let them sniff the barrel, drew out a couple glasses of the beautifully pink contents. It wasn't just me; they agreed that the wine was not only delicious, it was, well, frankly, aphrodisiacal.

I eventually bottled the wine and doled it out carefully, since it seemed to have this dangerous extra quality. Friends of mine came around the back door with their coat collars pulled up over their ears, begging for a bottle for a, uh, special date. It was also quickly evident that the wine was aging fast. The wine was best after a few months in its barrel, and then its quality began to fade fast. I bottled it quickly to save as much of the subtlety as I could, but there was no question in my mind that this stuff was going fast. So there was little sense in trying to save it. We drank it. I suppose I could have tried the other side of the culinary balance, bought a quarter ton of strawberries, tried to duplicate that nectar, but you know, a good part of the pleasure was the serendipity of it all, the gift of the fruit, the gift of the process, the gift of the results. Maybe I could have duplicated the taste, but that wasn't the point of my story when we leaned over that barrel and stuck our noses into the filler hole. The wine's story was not simply its exquisite taste but its adventure. And you can't buy that, or reestablish it once it's over.

SAUCE FOR THE GANDER

I suppose one could legitimately ask, "Sixty gallons of wine, five bottles per gallon, that's three hundred bottles, twenty-five cases, all of the same wine—isn't that boring, having that much of the same damned thing?" Well, yes, maybe. I suppose that's why I wound up giving so much of it away. But you simply take advantage of such things when you can. I feel the same way about nutrition. You're in the backyard, lying in a hammock, a mess of ribs smoking on the grill. You have a cold beer in your hand. Now, what are you going to have for supper? There's no doubt in my mind, and I submit that there wouldn't be a doubt in most men's minds: We're going to eat ribs and drink beer.

It's not my impression that that's the way a woman thinks. A woman is going to ask, as if she can't imagine how you could be such a doofus, "What about a salad? No vegetable? Just ribs and beer? Not even a slice of bread? That's it? Beer and ribs?"

She shakes her head in despair and goes to *her* kitchen to put together a lettuce salad, green beans, butter and bread, and something wholesome to drink. Her thinking is rational enough, at least on its surface: she is thinking in terms of balanced nutrition, vitamins, food groups, fiber, bulk, minimum daily requirements, and she deals with such considerations by carefully selecting foods that speak to what science tells her are those requirements.

A man does the same thing but in a slightly different way: he eats everything, all the time. Today it happens to be beer and ribs, tomorrow it could be green beans or, oh, asparagus. It's the difference between feminine tactical thinking—the short-term, situational response, problem solving—and masculine strategic thinking—the long term, the Big Picture, moving smoothly within the great and natural resonances of the cosmos. At this point, Linda usually points out that what she doesn't understand is that my nutritional strategy seems to focus so frequently on beer and ribs. Maybe even obsessively. In fact, she says, she thinks that given the freedom, all I'd eat is beer and ribs.

I don't believe that's true. Sooner or later I'd eat some sweet corn and maybe an avocado. I like pears and apples. I love bread. I'd eat other stuff sooner or later *because in the long run, I eat everything*. Cro-Magnons didn't have refrigeration or canning. They ate whatever came along, and they ate it all, and that's probably all they ate until something else came along. You kill a woolly mammoth, and man, you're going to eat woolly mammoth for weeks until the wang around that carcass gets to be just too much even for your in-laws, and by that time the saber-toothed tigers are getting a little on the troublesome side, so you move along, mostly because you heard a giant sloth fell out of a tree over by the next volcano, and your worthless brother-in-law managed to glom onto it, and he owes you one from the time he ate three-fourths of that three-toed horse you thought would last two weeks but was gone in three days, and so you eat sloth for a week. And then the acorns are ripe, and you eat those for a while. Mulberries give you the drizzles, but they're in season, and that happens only once a year, so today we eat mulberries. The system works. Name one Cro-Magnon who died of malnutrition.

Strategic cuisine is especially important when traveling. When I was in Monterrey, Mexico, I found the specialty was good bread, beer, and roast goat, so I ate bread, beer, and goat. In Saltillo, I found a great little winery, a street vendor who made terrific pork rinds, and a terrific pretzel shop, so . . . well, you get the idea. In the markets, I bought and ate whatever fruit was abundant, especially if I saw natives of the area eating it. The

only time I avoid what is available is when I make a point of not eating what I can get at home—good beef, McDonald's, Linda's cooking—when I am somewhere else. That's part of what travel is about, maybe most of what travel is about— eating things you don't eat at home.

Figure this way: this particular food evolved in this particular place, maybe, for a reason. Maybe people who ate this stuff here survived here because this stuff helped them survive here. People who ate other stuff, like McDonald's, died off. Sure, McDonald's is back here now, but who knows what the long-term effect will be? Ergo, if you want to survive *here*, eat what the folks *here* eat.

Foods at home in one context aren't always that great once they leave their original context, however. I came home from Mexico so taken with el cabrito, one long vacation at the cabin I bought a goat, butchered it, and decided to make some of my own goat barbecue, just like in Mexico. Well, things started badly when I bought the animal and loaded it; as I was leaving the farm, a young girl waved goodbye to me . . . actually the goat . . . and said softly, "Good-bye, Amanda." Oh man. Suddenly butchering was taking on all the delicacy of murder.

But I'm a man, and I'm a realist, and I did it. And I roasted the meat over an open fire, a little surprised that fifty or sixty pounds of live goat cuts down to about six pounds of useable meat. But I did it. And I went into town and told my pals what I was doing, and spent a fine afternoon drinking cold beer and thinking about the roast goat I was going to enjoy for supper. Then I went home about sundown and found . . . nothing. Someone had dropped in and eaten a mess of goat and didn't say so much as "Thanks, sucker." As I ate a hamburger in town later that evening, I asked myself, "Self, would you trust your loving, favorite dog Lucky to watch a steak for you while you drink beer in town all afternoon? No, I don't think so. Friends are friends, but men are men." And men and food are men and food, and friendship don't mean shit, as some of those very friends explained to me later.

THREE SQUARES

Okay, so much for serendipitous culinary opportunism. What about the other side of the issue, the scheduled meal? There are those too, but I would like to suggest that they don't have to be quite as rigid as they may seem. In my culture—white, mainstream, educated, middle class, rural, central Plains—we eat three meals a day, the largest in the evening. It doesn't have to be that way, and when Linda and Antonia aren't here, it isn't. I love to eat a huge breakfast— eggs, steak, pie, beer—and then coast the rest of the day, snacking, noshing, nibbling. Or a big noon meal (called "lunch" around here if it's relatively modest, "dinner" if it's more generous, evening meal being called "supper"; or sometimes "dinner" if . . . never mind), although more often than not, it is eaten at 5 P.M., which I consider a good idea, although it drives my East Coast friends who usually eat the evening meal at 9 P.M., bonkers, just as I am discomfited when I go to bed at 11 P.M. with a belly full of entree).

I am also not convinced that foods designated as evening food need to be evening food, or breakfast food breakfast food. In my family, when I was a kid, we considered French toast an entree. I was surprised when I found that others think of it as a breakfast dish. I am perfectly content with popcorn as a noon or evening meal. I like it for breakfast—it's cereal, after all!

When I was but a lad, I had the remarkable, wonderful experience of spending a long week in Paris with some people who knew how to do things. They understood that tourists need to see things like the Moulin Rouge, the Left Bank, the Eiffel Tower, that sort of thing, but there are also other experiences, unexpected adventures, that turn the normal, drab tourist visit into something special. They took us to Pont L'Eveque to sample that village's exquisite, stinky cheese, they took us to the chaos of the old Les Halles produce warehouse center at 3 in the morning to sample onion soup. We went to big fancy places, yes, but we also hit some back-door spots where no tourists had ever been before and probably haven't been since.

I was only a boy at the time, twenty-two years old, and hopelessly inexperienced in the ways of the world. My family's meal schedule was utterly inflexible. Breakfast at 7, lunch at noon, supper at 5. Period. To this day, my dad starts checking his watch if supper isn't on the table by 5:03. Before we got to Paris, we'd been cycling through Europe for two months on next to no money, so we had had our baptism in cultural diversity. We'd eaten a lot of unexpected foods, gone hungry, eaten what we could when we could. But our friends in Paris gave all this a new dimension. The man of the family worked a regular job, from 7 A.M. to 3 P.M., but he considered his second job to be us and our education. When he arrived home, he came with something new for us to try. I learned the trick of freezing gin for gin and tonics from him. Then we'd talk and drink and laugh while he relaxed, cleaned up, and outlined the evening's activities for us. About 8 we'd sit at the dining room table, and the cook brought in the meal, *one dish at a time.*

I had never seen that before. In my family, everything was there, and we chose and ate and got up and left. But here we talked about what we were eating, we talked about the wine, we talked. We ate a salad, and then sat back and talked and rested. Eventually a soup was delivered to our places, and we ate that, talked about it, enjoyed it, rested, talked, waited. Bread. Entree. Dessert.

About midnight we finished our meal. The secret of eating like that, however, is that the dishes are well spaced, and *it was at that point that our evening life began*. Unlike in New York, this was not thought of as the time to go to bed. At this point we got into the car and went out to a bistro, show, performance, to visit, whatever. We came home at 3 or 4 A.M., fell in bed, slept the sleep of the pure at heart, and woke up, as is civilized, about 10 in the morning, just in time for breakfast. A schedule of that sort is not a luxury everyone can afford. There are jobs, families, schedules that don't let us live like that. But there are also people who don't live like that who could. There are times when all of us could live like that and don't. Why? Because . . . well, just because.

One of the curious features of the white man's culture that constantly amuses, even puzzles, the traditional Native American is our reliance on the clock to tell us when to eat. The Clown Dancer, a feature of many Native American pow-wow performances, is often a white man, in a suit, with a tie, blue eyes, red lips . . . and a large alarm clock fastened to his belt with a chain, although he constantly carries it in his left hand, looking at it again and again, because it tells him, after all, when he's tired and when he's hungry.

I haven't carried a watch since the first years I began to spend time with the Omahas, thirty-five years ago. Yeah, we need to keep track of time to keep things going on schedule, but, as with food, there are lots of times when such rigidity is far from necessary. Before I married Lovely Linda, I used to wallow in the pleasure of coming to my cabin in the woods, down by Nebraska's Middle Loup River, and live for a couple weeks over the holidays without a clock or watch. Just live. Eat when I was hungry, sleep when I was tired, work when I wanted to work, drink when I wanted to drink. Talk about an idyllic life! The only glitch was once when I was working and eating—it was dark out but it was, after all, January, and stormy and it can be dark all day—and I decided to hike to town through the storm to have a brandy and maybe get some news about the storm from my buddies.

I was surprised to find the tavern closed—could the bad weather have closed things down? In fact, nothing was open, nothing was going, no one was around. Finally, I waded through the snow over to the service station, where I knew a clock was hanging on the wall behind the cash register. I scraped away the ice from the window and peered into the service station—and it was 3 o'clock. As it turned out, 3 A.M., but it might just as well have been 3 P.M. It didn't matter to me. I was a little disappointed to have spent so much energy to no avail but I did have a nice anecdote, after all, and I felt terrific that white man or not, I had managed to shrug off, even for this short time, the tyranny of the clock. Back at the cabin I mixed up some hot chocolate with peppermint schnapps, ate a bowl of Frosted Flakes, and finished reading *Centennial*. The next day I had a breakfast of pickled hard-boiled eggs and beer at the tavern late in what turned out to be the afternoon of the next day.

CALENDRAL CONSIDERATIONS

Ritual meals are visible signs of stability in this world where stability can be a rare commodity. Uncertainty is the only sure thing, it seems. I don't know if I'll still have a job at CBS next year at this time—in fact, there aren't any assurances that there will be a CBS next year at this time. Will there be a war? Will Linda be talking to me? Will friends abandon me, or will there be new ones? What will the weather have in store, and our finances? Who will be in charge, Republicans or Democrats—or will things be the same and no one will be in charge? Can't we be sure about anything?

Not even death and taxes have remained absolute: the medical and religious communities debate furiously about when life begins, and how and when it should end. Republicans throw every effort into releasing the rich from the burden of taxes on the theory that they will throw more dimes to the poor and then taxes won't be a burden to the poor even if they do have to pay more than the rich. So, if the poor show some good sense and get rich, they can forget about taxes. You just can't tell from one year to another if you're going to be paying or not. Can't we rely on a thing in this world?

Well, yes, we can. One thing *is* sure in America. There isn't a doubt in the world that we will eat turkey, cranberry sauce, stuffing, and pumpkin pie on Thanksgiving. Yeah, sure, I know—there's a family in your neighborhood that eats ham on Thanksgiving. And you eat apple pie because Aunt Grace can't stand the sight of pumpkin. I'm talking about millions and you're talking about dozens. The fundamental fact is that Thanksgiving is America's national holiday, THE national holiday, because on that day we all sit down and eat together. Not at the same table, and yet *at the same table*.

Thanksgiving doesn't have anything to do with history. Whatever popular history surrounds Thanksgiving is mostly horse pucky anyway. The Pilgrims didn't come here for religious freedom; they came here with the hope of imposing their own religious tyranny, and they gave it their best shot. Many still are. The Pilgrims were not the first here, or even among the first here; Santa Fe was a century old by the time the Pilgrims established

Plimoth. Pilgrims didn't wear those goofy black and white outfits, tall hats, and buckle shoes you see in television commercials or the paintings of Van Dyck or Rembrandt; the Pilgrims wore colorful clothes like you see in the paintings of Breughel.

And we don't eat that standard, ritual Thanksgiving meal for religious freedom, historical celebration, or cultural conservatism. Or nutrition. Or gratitude. That meal has no more to do with such things than Holy Communion has to do with yummy wafers and vintage wines. Thanksgiving is an affirmation of nationhood. On that day we are ritually one people, whatever our differences. Whatever changes, that remains the same. "How can it be such a . . . patriotic sort of thing without the Pledge of Allegiance and the flag and all that?" you ask? Well, because we all know that when it comes right down to it, the Pledge of Allegiance and the flag are symbols, now largely held hostage by superficial patriotic frauds; the substance of our oneness is eating together, and we do that on Thanksgiving. It'll be tough for scoundrels to steal that. Just yesterday I heard the fiction again that Thanksgiving is a distinctly and historically American holiday. It isn't. The English celebrated Harvest Home, precisely the same event, centuries before the Pilgrims called their Harvest Home a thanksgiving meal. The Pilgrims *continued* the tradition under difficult conditions. They deserve credit for that.

So, what does a man, an eating man, do on Thanksgiving? Eat and submit, that's what. No matter how you feel about your family or the in-laws, cranberries or pumpkin, this is the time to cave in. In fact, a real man sees this as an opportunity to celebrate the harvest, even if he didn't have one, and lard up for winter, even if he could winter-over pretty well without eating for a week or two at a time. Thanksgiving is a kind of national Holy Communion and it doesn't really matter if the host tastes like fish food and the wine is Mogen David.

In my family, even the humor of the holidays is traditional. Every year for as long as I can remember, and I can remember an easy fifty years, my father has recited the same three jokes at every Thanksgiving (and Christmas meal), two in English and one in German, our traditional language:

English Joke (remembering, please, that the English are not famous for their humor): "I'm going to eat every carrot [dramatic hesitation] and pea in this bowl."

English joke: "Pass the beef hearts."

"There are no beef hearts; these are beans."

"*Beef hearts* tomorrow!!"

German joke (remembering that compared with Germans, the English are hilarious): "Nah, wir hab'm ein Ent' aus dem Huhn gemacht." (In my familial dialect, "Ent'" can mean either "finish" or "duck"; thus, the translation is either "Well, we finished the turkey," or "Well, we made a duck out of the turkey."

These recitations are followed, invariably, by gales of laughter. Ah, Dad has once again told his jokes. Life is good. God is comfortably in His Heaven. All is well. Hahahahahahahahahaha.

I started with the easy holiday. Christmas is a little tougher. For one thing, it is a much more complicated holiday. I'm always amused when the theologically ignorant carp about putting the "real meaning" back in Christmas.

The "real meaning" of Christmas, the origins of that holiday, is the pagan observance of the winter solstice, the longest night, shortest day of the year. Thus, the lights, yule fire, birth of the "sun," all that. Far from such elements being a blasphemous intrusion on a Christian celebration, it's the other way around.

Forty years ago I found it remarkable that in Europe I would visit an ancient cathedral and take the tour into the basement, where one could see the ruins of a Roman or Celtic temple under the Christian edifice. And then I'd go to another church and do the same thing. And then another. Were there so many Roman and Celtic temples that every time the Christians built a church they stumbled on the ruins of an older place of worship? No, not at all. The Christians built their churches smack on top of the pagan structures, and for a variety of reasons. What better way to celebrate the victory of your faith than to humiliate, and eradicate, the others? If you put your church right on top of his church, and if he wants to worship on this sacred spot, then he's going to have to worship in your building, and before your god. And, after all, it is a sacred spot and has unknown powers. No sense in not taking advantage of that reality. So, early Christian fathers placed their churches precisely over the older places of worship, on the very same foundations.

Same thing with holidays. No one has the faintest notion when Jesus was born. But the pagans have a perfectly lovely celebration, and a biggie, on the winter solstice, so why don't we put our holiday right on top of theirs and take advantage of the fact that everyone will be celebrating anyway, and if they are going to celebrate any religious observations on that day, it will be ours, and besides, it is a sacred time and has unknown powers? No sense in not taking advantage of that reality.

There are still religious shards and shreds attached to the holiday. Linda, raised a Catholic, still serves fish on Christmas Eve, responding to an institutional aversion to flesh on a day when flesh is denied. Yes, and greed, envy, gluttony and all the rest of the vices prosper as they do at no other time of the year, but it doesn't take an anthropologist or theologian to look at what Christmas has become in America and realize it is more a practice of non-religious, even anti-religious behavior, than anything else. It certainly hasn't reached the stability or certainty of Thanksgiving, partially because of religious confusion (and diversity, what with Hanukkah happening at about the same time, and non-religious people celebrating with the same or more enthusiasm than the devout), but I see hints of Christmas's meal becoming the family celebration we often think Thanksgiving is.

Not in the traditional sense of Mom, Dad, and the 2.3 Kids, or even the modern precept of Mom and/or Dad, Significant Other, Mutual Child, Stepchildren (custodial parent permitting), and Grandparent Impoverished by Theft of Retirement Fund by Felonious CEO and/or Criminal Neglect of Congress to Develop National Health Program. I mean family in the wider sense of heritage, ethnicity, race, culture. Then such things as Hanukkah, Kwanzaa, Druidic solstice rites, even the atheist's rationalization of gift giving and deep-winter joy as a celebration of peace and brotherhood, fall easily into place and conflicts and confusion disappear (except insofar as some religious nuts wish such conflicts and confusion to continue, of course).

As I said, it's only a faint hint at this point, but I see around me, isolated as I am on America's central Plains, the extenuation of a long tradition to celebrate ethnicity at Christmas. Villages, towns, use late December as a time to remember, or re-invent, historical and ethnic roots. Norwegians and Swedes eat their lutefisk and lefsa, Czech kitchens smell of kolaches, pork roast, and dumplings, Danes whip up krumkage and glog, those most romantically lyrical of food names. I can't

help but wonder if it isn't all a reprise for Thanksgiving, a balance in the calendral paradigm: "Yes, exactly a month ago on Thanksgiving I celebrated my Americanness, but that's not to say I've forgotten my heritage. Here. I'll eat this historical, ethnic stuff to prove it."

It has become a part of a traditional Christmas among immigrant groups in America (and that includes most of us, after all) that even if a word of the native tongue is not heard through the entire rest of the year, grace for the Christmas meal is recited in Norwegian, German, Danish, Spanish, whatever. If Thanksgiving is a recognition of what we are (ironically, rather than a historical recognition of what we were, as we pretend), then Christmas is becoming, at least gastronomically, an admission of what we were (rather than of what we should be, as we again pretend). Isn't that interesting? Again, this is not a time to exert manhood. We are speaking to, and bowing to, much larger forces, buddies. Eat the lutefisk, fruitcake, kringele, almonds, and roll with the season. There'll be time for ribs another time.

I don't want to belabor the notion, but it is true that there are other culinary milestones scattered throughout the year to help us keep our psychic stability. You know what you eat on Easter—boiled eggs and ham, right? (Incidentally, remember what I said about Christians imposing their holidays on top of pagan holy days? Easter's a great example. The word "Easter" never comes up in the Bible. So, what's it mean? And what's with all the eggs and rabbits, anyway?

Ishtar was a very early and very widely respected goddess of sex and fertility. Spring, appropriately, was her time. Eggs . . . rabbits . . . you get the idea. I keep hoping that those zealots who insist we "put Christ back in Christmas" will eventually turn their attention to putting Ishtar back in Easter.)

MANY HAPPY RETURNS

Black-eyed peas on New Year's Day, potato salad and hot dogs on the Fourth of July, chocolates on St. Valentine's Day, excessive alcohol on St. Patrick's Day, pecan pie on my birthday . . . well, okay, that's another issue, but I thought I'd mention it anyway. We might, however, note that there are food traditions with such things as birthdays—when I ask for pecan pie for my birthday, Linda feels compelled nonetheless to bake a cake too. "You have to have cake for your birthday. I think it's in the Constitution somewhere." And I remember the scandal of a couple friends of mine a generation ago who shocked their proper and prominent families by having a chocolate wedding cake! Not just a chocolate groom's cake, which is symbolically acceptable, but a *chocolate wedding cake*. "Doesn't that white symbolize something?" was the parental question.

Here's where my theory about men being the heart of the ritual dimension of food threatens to fall apart. Or maybe it's just that men are more dedicated to the deeper, more spiritual dimension. Yeah, that's it— "deeper, more spiritual." A friend of mine is about to get married and he's baffled by the fury and flurry that surrounds his fiancée's preparations for the event. To my mind he captured magnificently the male understanding when, utterly confused, he said to me, "An open field, a keg of beer, a fire pit, and a pig . . . what else do you need for a wedding?"

One of the difficult tasks for children in learning about culture is the curious juxtaposition of death and food in the traditional funeral meal. I can remember asking the question myself: here we are, just returning from the graveside, and now we're supposed to sit down and eat a big meal with all these red-eyed people? Although among my German people the tradition was much more restrained than it often is among the more lively Czechs of my wife's family, or within the almost audacious wakes of the Irish and Italian, they are all to some dimension a reaffirmation of life, an insistence that although we have just had a painful reminder of the inevitability of death, there is also an inevitability to life. And its necessities. And pleasures. Let's eat. Ralph would want it that way.

While all of us probably deal with holiday foods, and most of us encounter at some time or another a wedding meal, few of us will have an opportunity to attend our own funeral meal. And yet, some do. One of the most interesting ceremonial meals of all confronts only a select, mercifully few—the last meal. When I used to spend long hours—weeks!—in my log cabin by the river, guests and I (mostly my family) devised a hundred games to pass the time, since we had no electricity. What fascinated me as I considered the process after the fact is how many of our activities focused on food and meals. We ate well enough. I'm not one to starve, and I have never considered hunger to be part of the charm of country or campsite living. We ate—probably more than we should have. But we still talked about food. And meals: If you could have a meal with any three living Americans, who would they be? Any three living human beings? Any three women? Any three fictional characters? Any three fictional characters from the works of Willa Cather? What's your favorite food and why? What is Chris's favorite food and why? What's your least favorite food? That sort of thing.

When the game came to food, it was one I've seen played not only in lonely, dark cabins, but in cars full of students on their way to a concert, families waiting for supper, friends hiking in the mountains: "If you knew you were about to have your last meal, and you could have anything you want, what would it be?" It's a curious notion, the idea that a set of tastes would even be of any concern to you, knowing you'd be in oblivion by tomorrow. (And if you're going to heaven, shouldn't you pretty much figure the chow's going to be pretty good when you get there, pretty much anything your heart desires anyway?)

I started keeping track. I once even asked a class of 150 students at the University of Nebraska to jot down what they might like for a last meal. Around here the entree is almost always steak. Side dishes and desserts tend to be those things that carry a cultural or emotional load for the unfortunate diner, contemplating death—Mom's pie, Grannie's home-canned beans, that sort of thing.

The whole idea is pretty macabre, you'll have to admit. It's the sort of choice that is hopelessly agonizing because you sincerely hope it's one you'll never have to make. "But if you *did* have to chose a last meal. . . ."

If it were up to me, I guess I'd just as soon eat out rather than ordering in.

FOOD AND FUSS

If I ever commit suicide, I'm going to do it by starving myself to death. That way I have plenty of time to change my mind.

—Dave Ratliff, in conversation,
1993

Nothing to do but work,
Nothing to eat but food,
Nothing to wear but clothes
To keep one from going nude.
. . . Nowhere to go but out,
Nowhere to come but back.

—Benjamin Franklin King Jr.,
The Pessimist

Pease porridge hot, pease porridge cold,
Pease porridge in the pot, nine days old;
Some like it hot, some like it cold,
Some like it in the pot . . . nine days old.

—Anonymous Pea Farmer

FOOD AND . . . MEDICINE

I realize I am breaking new anthropological, culinary, and literary ground here, writing about food as something to eat rather than something to prepare, to enjoy rather than study, considering the nature of food in terms of gender at a time when there aren't supposed to be any genders—or any differences between genders, at any rate—telling stories about food and me, a man.

But the point is not so much, as you should have seen by now, FOOD, or ME, or even MAN, but *stories*. Food is the stuff of our narratives, of our anecdotes, jokes, legends, and biographies. I'll say it again: Food has next to nothing to do with nutrition, taste, convenience, economy, or nature. Food is what we think about it and what it means and what it can do, sometimes in ways and directions utterly obvious to those of us who are eating it.

The problem is, when one breaks ground, one often has no idea what the ground over the next hill is going to look like. For example, I wrote the adjacent essay about gout for *Natural History* magazine at a time when I was wrestling mightily with that horrendous affliction. If you haven't had gout, you can't imagine what it's like. As I note, I usually manage to generate some indignation when I remark that a good case of gout puts childbirth to shame. The last time I was in my doctor's office, I took along a copy of the gout essay for his files and amusement. I showed it to his nurse. She laughed when I pointed out that she'd probably disagree with my evaluation of the pain of gout vis-à-vis birthing . . . and she said, no, that she is one of those rare women who has suffered both childbirth and gout, and gout wins by twelve centiagons (a centiagon is a unit of measure for pain, one centiagon being equal to the standard discomfort caused by a toothpick-size splinter driven a quarter inch up under one fingernail).

Gout is about food. It is caused by what we eat, and can be alleviated by what we eat.

Anyway, I got my usual quota of phone calls and letters about the article, all of them recommending different culinary cures for what is essentially a dietary affliction—plum pills, prunes, that sort of thing. Except for one lady, who sent me an excerpt from a new magazine called *Bottom Line/Personal,* as extracted from a report by Dr. T. B. C. Murrell of the University of Adelaide, Australia, *viz.,* "Having sex prevents men from getting gout. Gout is caused by high blood levels of uric acid that can crystallize to form painful deposits in joints. New finding: Increased sexual activity reduces uric acid levels in fertile men." Presenting the concomitant, implicit conclusion that *if you have enough sex, you can eat whatever you want without worrying about gout!!*

CHACUN À SON GOUT
(Source: from *Natural History* magazine,
November 1995, 104:11)

The closest I come to being rich is that I have gout, the rich man's disease. I can't imagine why gout has gotten the reputation of being an affliction of the rich; it can result from a high purine diet, which includes things like liver, beans, and chicken—not the first foods that come to mind when I think of Donald Trump's table. The impression that gout is a man's affliction, however, is more accurate: it is ten times more common among men than women. And from my personal experience (with the gout), I can tell you right now, it is also about ten times more painful than female problems like childbirth. I realize there may still be some debate about this, even though right now it's as plain as the big toe on my foot.

Which is where gout strikes more often than not—the toes. Other favorite spots for this agony are the knees, ankles, wrists, or fingers. In fact, gout occurs in precisely those places because that is precisely where it can cause the most discomfort.

What happens is your system loads up with purine. It has to go somewhere when there's no more room for it, so it forms uric acid crystals the general size and shape of a porcupine, barrel cactus, or the spiny head of a medieval mace. And there the crystals sit, *inside* your big toe, right where you have to walk on it. Or especially in my case, in my left knee, which I have come to rely pretty heavily on when I do things like walk. So, instead of having nice, smooth, slick surfaces working like ballbearings in all those places of your body that have to bend and flex, you got a handful of cockleburs.

You'd think maybe you could rub the swollen, red, throbbing joint with a good liniment, right? Ha! The very *idea* of touching that fiery, critical mass of agony is enough to send the sufferer into catatonic fits. Maybe a good dose of aspirin would be just the thing. Nope. Aspirin only makes the condition worse. How about a bottle of good wine or a couple cold beers? Wrong again—they make it worse, too. In fact, medical science has pretty well established that when it comes to gout, anything that sounds as if it might be good for it isn't.

So, what does medical science suggest? "Relax and elevate the affected joint." You are wallowing in pain and they want you to relax. "Apply ice." Buddy, you're not applying anything to that knee, and I mean it. "Don't wear tight shoes." Duh. "Watch your diet." That should do it. If I lay off liver and beans stewed in beer, the pain should go away in, oh, a year or two.

Thank goodness, there are alternative treatment systems. If you suffer from gout, you know that all you have to do is limp around a while and very quickly someone will recognize the symptoms—whimpering, pitiful eyes, immoderate language, the inclination to shoot anyone who comes closer than ten yards to your left knee—and offer up the usual folk remedies: cherries and charcoal.

Cherries strike me as a medication I can get along with. The traditional wisdom has it that any sort of cherries will do—sweet or sour, canned or fresh, cooked or raw. Recommended dosages run from "a handful" to "all you can eat." I like to think that cherries packaged in a way to facilitate the maximum intake by the patient, therefore, would be the best possible strategy. Cherry pie comes to mind. Or a handful of maraschino cherries floating in a tall, cold Tom Collins.

Charcoal is another matter. I tried charcoal briquets with milk and sugar, white gravy, chocolate frosting, gin, even a nice béarnaise sauce (one at a time, not all together), and I think I can say with some certainty that there's no condiment you can put on charcoal, no matter how good, that lends any noticeable gastronomic improvement to it. I even tried charcoal with cherries. Nothing.

Anyone who has seen me at work at my barbecue grill, however, knows there is more than one way to get charcoal into your system. When I'm cooking on the patio, an extra gin and tonic, a lively conversation with a buddy, or a good article in a good magazine almost guarantees at least one of the steaks or burgers sizzling over the *cooking* coals—maybe all of them—will develop a generous amount of charcoal around the edges, almost as if by its own volition. On one occasion our local volunteer fire department wound up helping me serve some hamburgers that spent a little too much time on the grill because I was tossing a Frisbee for our black Lab Thud ("The Name He Earned With His Head").

And so The Welsch Strategy for Battling the Gout begins to take shape—a Tom Collins with a couple extra cherries, a filet on the grill acquiring a blackened patina, cherry pie à la mode (preferably with an ice cream flecked with cherry bits), polished off with a snifter of kirsch. I don't know what all this will do for my throbbing knee, but it makes me feel better just to think about it.

Cherrybim

I have no idea where I got this recipe, but I started making this nectar when I was still in high school. You may find that as something of a surprise, since it is clearly alcoholic and I was clearly underage. My parents are German and are enlightened about such things. There may be an age limit for drinking alcohol in Germany by now, but the last time I was there—I think it was about 1987—there were still beer machines, very much like soft drink dispensers in this country, where you dropped in your coin, and you got your bottle of beer, no questions asked. In fact, I got a lot of mileage out of the joke that my favorite German beer was *Einwurf*. (*Einwurf* is the word over the slot in beer machines, sort of like "Insert Coin Here." Again, an example of razor-edge German wit.)

I sat in *Weinstuben* (wine parlors) on Sunday afternoons and watched well-dressed families—Mom, Dad, Sis, Buster—come in and order a little smoked salmon, a small loaf of fresh bread, or local cold sausage and cheese and maybe two or three half bottles of wine. They ate, drank, and discussed the qualities of the cheese, sausage, bread, . . . and the wine. The children were learning about food, about wine, and most of all, about how people behave in civilized contexts. Damn the bluenoses and drunks who destroy such potentials in our nation! Damn them, damn them, damn them.

My old man, God bless him, sat me down early on and told me, and I quote, "When you think you're ready for a beer, my boy, it's in the refrigerator. Understand?" I understood. I never saw Dad drink more than one beer at a time, maybe two when we were fishing with uncles or at a wedding. But in those days there was beer in the fridge. And I remember the hot summer day, after mowing the lawn, when I came in the house and made my move. I was, I suppose, fifteen—a big, strapping boy just finishing a man's job. I went to the front room, where Dad was sitting in his eternal chair, doing his eternal crossword puzzle. "Lawn's done," I said.

"Great," he said, without even looking up.

"Think I'll have a beer," I said, choking and stuttering only a little.

He grunted in a neutral sort of way, still without looking up. I went to the kitchen and opened the refrigerator. I took out a bottle of beer. I opened it. I walked through the front room in order to make the situation as unambiguous as I could: I was having a beer. I was dirty and sweaty and needed to go outside rather than sit on Mom's furniture, but I thought better of sitting on the front porch, being about six years too young to drink the beer in my hand. I went to the backyard and sat, like a man, at our patio table and enjoyed a beer. And just what the hell is wrong with that?

Two summers later I was out on the front porch lighting firecrackers, so it must have been late June. A new neighbor kid, a typical nine-year-old pain in the ass of course, came drifting over. My idea of hell was having a nine-year-old live next door, and here he was, his air force dentist father having just been transferred to Lincoln and having the incredible bad manners to move next door to us. The kid pestered me every day the first five days they lived there, just hanging around—the precise single thing a man about to go to college doesn't want hanging around. I was about to fold up my firecracker games and leave him sitting there when he said, "Mom is coming to join us next week."

"Mmmm," I mumbled, utterly unenchanted.

"My sister's coming to join Dad and me here next week. Wanna see a picture of her?"

"Not really." All I had to do was look at this chubby little freckle farm to know that his sister was going to be even more of a pest in my life.

"Here she is," he said, whipping out a picture.

"Mmmm," I said, utterly without interest.

Then I glanced at the photo in his hand. Holy shit!! "This is your sister?" I asked.

"Yep," he said. I checked the photo to make sure it wasn't one of those Hollywood starlet things they stick in new billfolds. It wasn't. "That's her, all right. She doesn't like it, though, because she thinks it makes her look skinny."

I put my arm over the boy's shoulder. "Hey, how would you like to have the rest of this box of firecrackers? There you go. What's your name again? And you'll be living right here, in that house, about ten feet from our house, do I have that right? How about a dollar? Would you like a dollar? And your sister's name is . . . ?"

"Suzy O'Morrow," he said.

Suzy O'Morrow. Suzy O'Morrow.

That summer I worked on a road construction gang, shoveling hot asphalt and running a pneumatic jackhammer nine hours a day. I was a bronzed Adonis. And I was invited to join a fraternity. I mean, I was on top of the world. I don't remember much about Suzy O'Morrow, but I do remember she was a college freshman's dream. And I remember she quickly dumped me and took up with Bob Anderson, because he had a red convertible.

That taught me a lot, as you can imagine, but the best part was Suzy O'Morrow's father. A day or two before Suzy O'Morrow came to Lincoln, I came home from my construction job, soaked in sweat, black from tar, exhausted by the backbreaking work. As I crawled out of my car, Mr. O'Morrow—I think he was a captain with the air force—called to me from his front porch, "Looks like you've had a long day."

"You said it," I replied, or something like that.

He introduced himself, apologized for his obnoxious son, and asked me if I would like to join him in a cold drink. My folks weren't home, so I apologized for my filthy condition—which he dismissed—and accepted his invitation. And we had a gin and tonic. My first. Now, if you have ever had a good gin and tonic on a miserably hot day, much like the English colonists who invented it in sweltering colonial India, you know how good those things can be. And again, a mature, intelligent adult showed me how mature, intelligent people use alcohol. Ignorance does not serve anyone well, I assure you.

Anyway, that's what my experience with alcohol has always been. (Okay, there were a few bad times, but some people get carried away with coffee or jelly beans now and then, too.) So, Mom and Dad understood when I explained that I had run across this recipe, called Cherrybim, and I wanted to try it as a Christmas drink. And they got me the necessary ingredients to make a pint, and we enjoyed it mightily six months later at Christmas.

Here's what you do.

Get a mess of clean, fresh cherries. I have used both pie cherries and black cherries. I think this would be great with sand cherries or chokecherries, and now that I think of it, next summer I'll give them a try. Get a container that will give you plenty of room for those cherries and about that much more other stuff you're going to chuck in there. A big jar will do. You need to have something that can be closed tightly. I have a two-gallon glass jar that once held jerky up at the tavern I'm going to use next time; I talked the bartender out of it by promising to buy my whiskey for the recipe from him.

Put an inch or two of clean cherries in the bottom of your container. Next, put down a thin layer of sugar cubes. Toss in a couple whole cloves. Put in another layer of cherries, and another layer of sugar cubes, and a few cloves. Do this until your jar is loosely filled. Don't tamp down or pack the cherries and cubes because you want plenty of room for the next, main ingredient—whiskey.

Now, pour bourbon—it doesn't have to be a great whiskey, an ordinary bar whiskey will do—over the cherries, sugar, and spice until your container is full. Don't stir or agitate this stuff. You want as much sugar as possible to stay high up in the container so there is as close to an equal distribution as you can get. Seal the jar and let it sit quietly in a dark, cool place a half year or so. (This is a superb winter, especially Christmas, drink, so you may want to start thinking of it about the time cherries start showing up on your tree or in your grocery store.)

When you again open the jar, you will find that a wonderful cherry taste and aroma has permeated the whiskey and you have a liqueur that can't be beat. Absolutely delicious. And you will find that the cherries have taken on the stronger tastes of the whiskey! So you can eat a few cherries (remember: they're good for your gout!) or, my favorite, *pour a generous tablespoon or two of them over ice cream.* You'll think you've died and gone to Heaven.

. . . AND HISTORY

We know about food and sex. . . . There is no end of foods reputed to increase sexual prowess—green M&Ms, champagne, oysters. But how about food and the scholarship of history? Frontier archaeologists don't make much of a fuss about it, but oyster tins sometimes serve as important research indices. Imagine this scenario: you know from military records that hog farms, a delicate military term for whorehouses, were required by a discipline-prone commander to be, oh, say, five miles away from the fort. You're an archaeologist looking for material evidence of how soldiers of the period lived. You take a map and a string representing five miles on the scale; you draw a circle exactly five miles from the fort. It stands to reason that whorehouses would have been placed pretty close to that line, a man having his needs, after all.

Then you hike that circle on the ground, observing carefully all buildings or building ruins along the route. You find a farm building, used for livestock and tractor storage, that has stalls a little larger one might normally expect for horses, a little smaller than you'd plan for tractors. Is this perhaps a frontier "mustang ranch" and the stalls actually "cribs"? This might be a great place to look for artifacts, since it stands to reason that in this particular place, a lot of soldiers shed a lot of gear at one time or another. There are some old garbage mounds behind the shed, so you dig into one of them. You find smallish oval or round tins with the tops cut open by a sharp object having been drawn across them in a cross. Well, the openings are already a clue, because this is the expedient way soldiers often opened ration cans. You find a can with an embossed label on a lid; you straighten out the lid enough to read the label, and it says, "Smith's Famous Oysters."

Oh yeah, it was a whorehouse, and if you continue your hunt, you'll find buttons, pins, liquor bottles, pistols (often dropped down outhouse openings, by the way), corset stays, and ladies' fine ornamentals. Oysters were sold and served at such establishments as an aid for improving . . . er . . . performance, as a kind of antidote for the saltpeter tradition tells us is used liberally to season military food and reduce tension in the barracks. That being the case, there'd be no worse waste of money than to travel all this way, put down your hard-earned soldier's wages, and then, well, fall short of the mark, so to speak. So you buy a tin of oysters from the big, nasty lady in charge of the operation—just in case.

Medicine, history, romance . . . who can say what influence food can have on us? I got a letter from Jim Harrison just yesterday in which he said he once ate five deer hearts and won five hundred dollars in a poker game. Coincidence? Yeah, sure. Now we have to consider the possible wisdom of the nineteenth-century soldier avoiding gout by eating a regular dose of oysters so he then can have better sex—an example of food applied as medicine. And then food as a tool of historical research. The mind boggles, doesn't it?

AND EVERYTHING ELSE

How about food and politics? George Bush tried to enchant the unwashed masses and disguise his plutocratic heritage by crunching lowly pork rinds; Ronald Reagan scarfed jelly beans (but gourmet beans, let's remember); and Bill Clinton eats too much of everything plebian. Forget the candidates' sexual exploits and legal entanglements! I want to know what they eat!

Or don't eat. How about food and survival? Can we even trust ourselves to eat when it is a matter of staying alive? While others swoon over the courage and foresight of our pioneer forefathers, I tend to think of them as a bunch of ignorant louts. Few who came to the frontier came because they were well informed. They came here because they didn't have the foggiest notion what they were getting into, and once they got into it, they didn't even have the common sense to grope their way out. So they stayed and were pioneers. Oh boy, some heroes!

On the Plains frontier, settlers butchered, as was traditional, in the fall, to save having to feed one more animal during the winter and with the hope that cold weather would help preserve the meat during the long, cold, hungry winter. A beef carcass was hanged in the barn where cuts could be removed, taken to the house, and cooked as the need arose. The unpredictable Plains weather, however, meant that invariably, every winter had its warm spells, during which the meat spoiled or was infected by maggots. (A pioneer account suggested that there was a system by which settlers could avoid getting skippers—maggots—in their hanging meat during the spring: "Eat it during the winter.")

Meanwhile, over the hill, in the Indian village, folks were smoking and drying meat, producing a good, nutritious, sanitary food that would keep for years. Nowadays, a white man will pay a dollar for a fraction of an ounce of jerked beef in a tavern, but on the frontier a family might starve rather than eat—ugh!—Indian food. Families did indeed starve rather than eat—ugh!—Indian food. There are a few accounts in which frontier households stooped to Indian food during periods of extreme famine: groundnuts stolen from prairie mice nests, cattail root flour, wild turnips, arrowhead tubers. The reports invariably note that the food was actually quite good . . . but that the family reverted to decent white food as soon as conditions improved, having thus admittedly learned nothing. They ignored the reality that Indians lived comfortably for millennia here on the Plains, eating the bounty nature provided, insisting instead to try to inflict their own exotic food systems on an unaccepting geography and history. Dimbulbs!

One of the features of Native American culture that drew me deeply and personally into it thirty-five years ago was how food is distributed within the Indian community. I guess this is a matter of food and economics. It is simple enough, and logically indisputable: those who have food at any particular time, share it; those who need food, accept it. Men prepare and serve feast food among the Omaha Tribe, which, as I've mentioned before, is my tribal association. I think that is part of the gender balance, too: it is a mother's job to make sure her family is fed. It is a man's job to make sure his village is fed. As I've noted before, food is prepared, where possible, in ways that facilitate flexible distribution. At mealtime all food is brought to the center of the gathering, where it is blessed; then men take the huge boxes, cauldrons, tubs, and bags and start their rounds, putting equal proportions of everything on every plate.

If a child is asleep at the time of food distribution, his or her plate is set out with the rest. Everyone gets a share. All the food, or almost all the food (more about that in a second), is distributed. If there is a little food, everyone gets a little. That seems fair. If there is a lot, everyone gets a lot. Often more than can be eaten. That's okay, too. Take home what can't be eaten on the spot. (Except at a Pawnee funeral feast, where everything is supposed to be eaten, since you are also eating for the dead.) So, families with lots of children, where food is most needed, get the most food. Single people, who don't need much, don't get a lot. People who can afford food, provide food. When they're not enjoying fat times, well, they know they'll be eating anyway, because whoever *is* doing all right will be bringing food to the feast.

There are sometimes leftovers that cannot be easily distributed—tubs of soup, for example, or a hog's head. Whoever would like to take such leftovers is welcome to them. There is no shame in it; it is simply a process of treating the food with respect, and thereby feeding the hungry. The only question that comes up as the poorest of these poor take an extra share of the feast food is "Can I take that home for you, Grandma?" If Dillinger—or was it Willie Sutton?—was a wit for declaring that he robbed banks because that's where the money is, then why do we have such a hard time figuring out that food should be where there is hunger? Compare economics like that with the supply-side economics of some idiots in Washington, D.C.

Forget scholarly dimensions of food. How about what it does in our personal lives? I once concluded a relationship because I was eating in this froo-froo salad place at the behest of the young lady, finishing a greenish meal with a piece of carrot cake. Carrot cake is okay, but to my mind it is only redeemed by cream cheese frosting. Actually, that's true for all cake. Cake is cake, but frosting is FROSTING. For forty years I ate my cake in the same, hopelessly adolescent (if not childish) way: I got rid of the cake, leaving a ridge of frosting standing on my plate, which I then enjoyed at my leisure, carrying with me from the table mouth-echoes of its richness.

Well, this woman and I were finishing up the meal, as I said, and I was well into my carrot cake, when she said, looking past me toward the front of the restaurant, "Look there! Isn't that Dave Wishart?" Dave Wishart is an old friend of mine, the son of the John and Muriel Wishart, whom I mentioned earlier. So I turned and looked. I didn't see Dave, so I looked more intently. I turned back to my lunch companion and said, "I don't see Dave Wishart."

"I must have been mistaken, then," she smiled coyly.

I turned back to my cream cheese frosting. But it was gone. She had eaten it. And my whole goddamn day was ruined. And our relationship was ruined. My first wife had an affair with my best friend, and that seemed pretty painful at the time, although I am reminded of the guy who comes into the tavern visibly downcast and explains, "My best friend, Bob, just ran off with my wife," to which the bartender says, "I thought I was your best friend." The newcomer replies, "Well, you were until Bob ran off with my wife." That deceit and betrayal was nothing compared to the theft of the frosting from my carrot cake. I include this story here not so much by way of instruction to you, the reader, as example for my manuscript reader, my wife, Linda. Just as surely as food leads to sex and romance, it can destroy same.

Sex is sex but food is food. If you doubt me, ask my dogs. They don't growl when I hit them with that bucket of cold water, but they're not yet ready to share their food with me. We humans are ready to share our food . . . in keeping with certain ground rules. You may find religious mendicants who are willing to take on the burden of giving up sex for all their lives, but few offer to surrender their food.

AN AFTERWORD

My life, my joy, my food, my all the world . . .
—SHAKESPEARE,
King John, 1596

This stuff is so damned good, I almost hate to eat it!
—DANNEBROG VOLUNTEER FIREMAN'S
PICNIC, 1976

Eat, eat, eat!

—EVERY MOTHER WHO'S EVER LIVED,
DAILY

I know people who love to cook. They take real pleasure in buying the ingredients at the market, in preparing them in the kitchen, in bringing them to the table. I think I can understand that kind of joy. It's a very generous spirit. God bless them. Give me more friends like that—Dee, Jay, Bertha, Sally, Jake, Harriett, Sue . . .

Me, I'm the sort of person who makes that kind of person happy. I like to eat. While excess has its pleasures, Heaven knows, my joy in ingestion is not simply an issue of gluttony:

one spring I found and ate a single morel mushroom I found down by the river on my farm. It was no less a pleasure to me for being a morel rather than a truffle, no less satisfying for being one than a bushel. I'm currently in the process of losing some weight—with luck, a lot of weight. Does this mean I am enjoying food less? Far from it! I enjoy what I am eating these days all the more.

For one thing, I like tastes. Whatever *they* are. Tastes are mysterious. We can say, "The car sounded as if there were a gunnysack of loose cans under the hood and a box of hungry cats in the trunk," and communicate a pretty good idea of how that automobile sounds. We can say, "The house looked as if it hadn't been lived in since I was a boy," and I can see the building in my mind's eye now. We can say, "His hands were as rough as sandpaper, and he smelled like the clay from which he made his bricks." You know this man; you've met him.

But what can we say of food? That's the mystery. Tell me what your mother's rye bread tastes like. No, try it, really: what does it taste like? Can't do it, can you? Tell me about the perfume of good wine, without using all those empty adjectives conventional to wine snobbery. How does good quality, well-prepared pasta feel in your mouth? Describe the sensation of drinking champagne to me in such a way that I'll be able to taste it myself, or even come close to knowing what you're saying. Can't be done. It's like trying to describe an accordion without using your hands.

When it comes right down to it, about all we can do to communicate to fellow human beings about food is to say, "Here—try some of this." And then we begin to see food for what it really is.

We really are, as the Beatles said, what we eat, and more precisely, as George Schwelle wrote, "We eat what we are."

Food is symbol and meaning, our soul, substance, and heart. Nothing is at the same time as common to all of us as food and yet nothing is so personal, so public, and so intimate.

And nowhere can the joy of life be more clearly seen and understood than in food. A piece of licorice that brings back rich memories of prizes from a grandfather's pocket, a rare wine laden with connotations of a time past, a strawberry from a lover's fingertips, a breakfast trout's filet garnished with a Lakota prayer of gratitude for the fish's sacrifice to feed our own flesh, the tenth glass of beer downed in laughter upon the return of an old friend, a stale cracker eaten under an ancient cedar with a good friend, an ordinary meal recalled years later as the first of thousands taken with one's mate . . .

That's what food's all about, and it's not small potatoes.

A BRIEF BUT RICHLY ORNAMENTED BIBLIOGRAPHY

The perfect recipe is what you get when you ask your grandmother how she makes that great bread of hers: "Vell, you takes as much flour as you wants, und adds enough water to make de dough, you know, just right. Den you add a pinch of salt and a pudja of shukar. You kneads it until it is ready to rise und you let it sit in de varm place until it's rised. You beats it down and kneads it again, and den you does dat one more time just the same again. You heats your oven until it is ready, puts de bread in until it is baked, and der you are."

Huh?

Problem is, your grandma is right, and the recipe books are wrong. The books make it sound like a mere matter of mixing the exact amounts of things together and treating them in precisely one way and then you have success. It just doesn't work that way. Your best bet is to find a local church recipe book, because it is likely to have real food in it—food

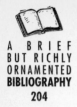

you are familiar with. Linda has a few on her shelf. I'm not saying these are any better than any others; these are just examples of what I have in mind.

Unbearably Good: Favorite Recipes from Assumption Parish [of Dwight, Nebraska]. Kearney, Neb.: Morris Press, 1994. Lots of Czech and German recipes, reflecting the ethnic nature of the community—and our tastes, incidentally.

Saint Patrick's Catholic Church Centennial Cookbook [of Lincoln, Nebraska]. Audubon, Ia.: Jumbo Jack's Cookbooks, 1993. Again, this cookbook contains recipes reflecting our tastes, since Linda and I are both from lower-class ethnic neighborhoods in Lincoln.

These days nonreligious communities are also publishing cookbooks. Linda did the artwork for the cover of *Dannebrog Country Kitchens: Recipes from the Heart* (Kearney, Neb.: Morris Press, 1994). Unfortunately, most of the recipes are Danish, which means the pastries and finger foods are good but the rest of the food is pretty bland to the palate and too fancy to the eye for my idea of fixin's and vittles.

As the fashion for ethnic pride and awareness has grown, so too has the cookbook inventory. My mother had to be forced to fix our traditional German foods during my youth—*runzas, schnitzsupp', grebel,* and *rivelkueche,* for example—because for a long time there, German foods were not exactly in vogue, if you catch my drift. (In fact, sauerkraut, a staple in our diet, was patriotically renamed victory cabbage, which says a lot more about the idiocy of patriotism than it does about sauerkraut.) Now, even my people are producing cookbooks! Most notably *Kueche Kochen* by the American Historical Society of Germans from Russia (Lincoln, Neb.: 1973). See, if you're a Rooshen, this is your cookbook. If you're Hispanic or Czech or Polish, obviously you're going to find another to your taste. You get the idea.

Linda's book *Favorite Recipes of the Nebraska Czechs* is published by The Nebraska Czechs of Wilbur (Wilbur, Neb.: 1968). Her copy is covered with notes and stains, and the pages are tattered and dog-eared. Good sign in a cookbook.

If ethnic cookbooks speak to men because they contain predominantly peasant recipes, and real men are predominantly peasants, then historical, frontierish cookbooks (not historical rich folks or aristocratic cookbooks) are suitable for male cooking, because the recipes tend to be for survival foods—fast, easy, basic, nutritious, zesty, solid, generous, and flexible. Just like us.

The ones on my shelf are:

Wes Medley's *Original Cowboy Cookbook* (Cairo, Neb.: Record Printing, 1989). A great little no-nonsense cookbook, this doesn't include "Son-of-a-Bitch Stew" but does have "A Hell of a Breakfast."

Sam Arnold's *Frying Pans West Cookbook* (Morrison, Colo.: Sam Arnold, The Fort, 1969) is pretty thin to be useful but is still worth having on your shelf, since it is clearly men's food meant for men-type cooks.

Stella Hughes must be quite a lady, since she knows about men and food, as demonstrated generously in her *Chuck Wagon Cookin'* (Tucson: University of Arizona Press, 1974). She does include "Son-of-a-Bitch Stew," not to mention "Bastard-in-a-Bag," "Ox-gall Soap" [sic], and "Grandma's Salve for Everything."

Less useful but still referred to now and again in my summer kitchen is Kay Graber's *Nebraska Pioneer Cookbook* (Lincoln, Neb.: University of Nebraska Press, 1974).

And if I might be so presumptuous, I'd like to recom-

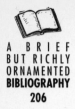

mend a couple of my own publications. *Treasury of Nebraska Pioneer Folklore,* my very first book, published in 1966 (Lincoln, Neb.: University of Nebraska Press), has a chapter on pioneer cookery and recipes collected by WPA fieldworkers from genuine Plains pioneers during the 1930s. Popcorn pudding is a special favorite of mine.

Lovely Linda and I put together a beautiful book titled *Cather's Kitchens: Foodways in Literature and Life* (Lincoln, Neb.: University of Nebraska Press, 1987) that includes a lot of pioneer recipes, although from more sophisticated kitchens than those on the earliest frontier. I had written a couple academic papers on how effectively Willa Cather used foods as literary devices, demonstrating that she knew her way around food as well as the English language. A former student of mine, who had become director of the Cather Museum in Red Cloud, Nebraska, mentioned to me one day that she had in the museum's archives the actual cookbooks from Willa Cather's childhood home. Her mother's cookbooks. And a file of her family's recipes. EEEEEK! That meant I could actually match the foods she mentioned in her magnificent books with the real stuff, the actual food itself.

Which is what Linda and I did. When she mentions plum jam, by God, we could show you exactly what she had in mind, what she had grown up knowing as plum jam—Willa Cather's *mother's* plum jam! Where there were holes in the recipe files, we sought recipes from other members of her family, from the immediate region around Red Cloud, and from ethnic groups identical to those she referred to in her works. I think it was a neat idea. And the book did well. With these recipes, you not only have early American examples of cookery, you are immersing yourself in some pretty intellectual stuff—a kind of process of sophistication and erudition by ingestion. You serve the dish, and when someone says, "This is interesting. Where did you get the recipe?" you tell them the story I just told you above. Your lady friend or dining companions will think you're a real intellectual, and all you're doing is eating. See? I've thought about this.

And here are a couple of the more widely available sources that might help you in one way or another:

Joy of Cooking, by Irma S. Rombauer and Marion Rombauer Becker (New York: Bobbs-Merrill, 1931), is a cookbook worthy of reading. It is the best cookbook there is. It has all the fancy stuff like Pâté à Choux and Oysters Rockefeller, but it also has oxtail soup and, no kidding, peanut butter sandwiches (*avec tomates* and *sur du bacon*). The recipes are economically brief but literate. This is a fun book to browse through. Ever since I first started cooking—insofar as I have ever cooked—forty years ago, I have used this book. I bought a copy for my thirteen-year-old daughter last Christmas. Her husband will thank me. If you can have any cookbook, have this one; if you can have only one cookbook, this is it.

White Trash Cooking, by Ernest Matthew Mickler (Berkeley: Ten Speed Press, 1986), is a favorite of mine. Linda was a little troubled when my son gave her a copy of this book. She's a woman, and he's a man. She doesn't think of herself as white trash; he knows he is. All men are. In some ways, this is the perfect cookbook for men. It has great recipes and deals with ingredients and processes men understand and appreciate. The language is annoying and artificially regional—downright cute, sometimes—but maybe it's okay, if you happen to be a man in Georgia. The language doesn't work in Nebraska, but the recipes do.

I used to have a copy of the *Better Homes and Gardens*

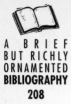

Cookbook, a loose-leaf, red-and-white-checkerboard book that I really liked and used a lot. I lost it in the divorce, however, and I never got another copy. Next time I'm in a bookstore, I'm going to look around for it.

My copy of George Leonard Herter and Berthe Herter's *Bull Cook and Authentic Historical Recipes and Practices* (Waseca, Minn.: Herter's, 1960) is battered and worn. This thing may not even be in publication. You may have to find it at a Goodwill store or the estate auction of some grizzled old bachelor. Herter's was—maybe still is—a mail-order sporting goods outlet, sort of the granddaddy of L.L. Bean and Cabela's. And while I never met George Leonard, you don't have to read very far in his literary work (I especially enjoy *George the Housewife*) to figure out this guy is a genuine American original. Here's where you find out how to dress a snapping turtle (no, no, not that way—gut and clean!), buy wieners, or prepare Duck Genghis Khan and Doves Wyatt Earp. There are also helpful chapters like "The Indian Method of Removing Hair from Rabbit and Squirrel Carcasses" and "Red Pepper Good for Radiation."

It's not the sort of thing I suppose your casual male cook would find interesting or useful, but I couldn't do without my copy of Frank Ashbrook's *Butchering, Processing, and Preservation of Meat: Cattle, Hogs, Sheep, Game, Poultry, Fish, a Manual for Home and Farm* (New York: Van Nostrand Reinhold Co., 1955). If you are going to get into butchering, curing and smoking hams, making sausage, that kind of thing, this is the book you need.

Knowing how Villard Books operates—they've published a couple of my books—Chris Maynard and Bill Scheller's book *The One! the Only! Guide to Cooking on Your Car Engine: Manifold Destiny* (New York, 1989) probably isn't in print anymore, but you may be able to find it in a used bookstore somewhere. This thin volume is an expansion of the notion I explored earlier of cooking on your car engine. I was a little miffed when these guys came up with a book about something I'd been doing for years, but that's the way it goes. If nothing

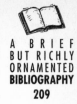

else, this book is a great conversation piece for your bathroom when guests come by.

Calvin Trillin is my favorite foods book writer. (Jim Harrison would be, but he hasn't done a foods book yet, and probably never will, considering the kind of money he's making off movie scripts.) Trillin, for one thing, is a great writer, and second, he's a great eater. He knows his way around fancy food in New York, but he grew up eating ordinary food in Kansas City, and it shows. I once had the incredible good fortune of enjoying an excellent, long meal sitting between Charles Kuralt and Calvin Trillin, two of my favorite eaters and writers in this world. It was like Heaven. Read Trillin's books, and you'll understand. I recommend his collection *The Tummy Trilogy* (New York: Noonday Press, 1994). It contains his three best long food essays, "American Fried," "Alice, Let's Eat," and "Third Helpings." THIS IS NOT A RECIPE BOOK. IT'S BETTER THAN A RECIPE BOOK. IT'S A FOOD BOOK.

Finally, I strongly recommend that you visit your local bookstore and see what is current on their cookbook shelves. Check the Self-Help and Diets sections. Look for books like George Mateljan's *Cooking Without Fat* (Irwindale, Calif.: Health Valley Foods, 1992). Look through it, laugh at it. If anyone invites you to a party and gushes, "And guess what! George Mateljan is going to be there and do some cooking for us," you'll know to stay the hell away. What this guy knows about food is precisely what I don't need.

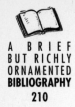

Better yet, if you're courting, and you wind up in a beautiful young woman's home, much as I described early on in this book, and things move along nicely, and she slips away to get into something (gasp, choke) "more comfortable" and says maybe when she comes back, you'd like to go to her bedroom and see the new bed quilt she bought earlier in the day, before you do anything else (like get comfortable yourself) take a quick inventory of her kitchen. You can forgive her the empty, ice-locked fridge, you can forgive her the yogurt and rice cakes (she's a woman, after all), but if you find books like *Cooking Without Fat*, before you accept her invitation to see her new bed quilt, ask her about her ideas on good food. Okay, right after you see the new quilt, then you can ask her about her ideas on good food. If you find *White Trash Cooking* or *The Joy of Cooking*, fire at will. If she has *Butchering, Processing, and Preservation of Meat: Cattle, Hogs, Sheep, Game, Poultry, Fish, a Manual for Home and Farm* or anything by Calvin Trillin on her coffee table, propose first and check her new bed cover later.

ACKNOWLEDGMENTS

Where does one start thanking those who have contributed to a lifetime of enjoying and learning and thinking about food? That would include everyone from the lady who used to take drive-in orders at the Tastee Inn and Out to the chef at the Cornhusker Hotel's Renaissance Room, from my Lovely Linda to German, Omaha Indian, and Norwegian aunts, long gone, from the creatures (from lettuce to sharks) who've given their lives to keep this organism of mine from going lo! these sixty years to the gods who've toyed with my appetites and gratifications, all the eaters, and all the cooks. That's some assignment.

In the case of his essay, I owe special thanks to Jim Harrison. Everyone wants him to write an introduction for a book; he wrote one for this book, and all it is costing me is a ham every Christmas for the rest of my ham-smoking life. I consider it a bargain. My daughter Joyce, although she is a vegetarian, patiently and carefully read this omnivorous manuscript, offering lots of suggestions, many of them not at all insulting. Mauro DiPreta is one of those rare editors who

ACKNOWLEDGMENTS
212

understands not only the business of bullying manuscripts but of humoring writers; his encouragement of my spirit means as much to me as his careful treatment of my words. (Any errors or obscurities in these pages, by the way, are Mauro's responsibility; write him, not me.)

There have always been jokes about agents in show biz and publishing, but you won't hear any from me. Tom Connor is more like a partner and friend than literary agent in my life. I am indebted to him (but am not at all interested in raising his percentage of the net, in case that's what he's thinking).

Saying grace before meals gives me some discomfort because my Omaha Indian brother, Buddy Gilpin, once told me that among our people, the Omaha, the ideal is for every moment of life to be a prayer of gratitude. Taking a few seconds, therefore, to say thanks is not even close to that noble ideal. I feel the same way about thanking Linda here. She is everything. So is it perhaps trivial to thank her for a little something within all that everything? Scarcely a moment of my life passes without me wondering by what miraculous grace she is my mate, and so read this as just one more of those moments: thank you, my Linda, my Lily.

I want to thank Jay Leno for inviting me to be on his show to talk about this book, which I'm pretty sure he'll want to do, and Claudia Schiffer for . . . well, she knows.

Mostly I'm grateful to all those responsible for me never having gone hungry for very long in my life.